Does Nonfiction
Equate Truth?

Does Nonfiction Equate Truth?

Rethinking Disciplinary Boundaries through Critical Literacy

Edited by
Vivian Yenika-Agbaw,
Laura Anne Hudock, and
Ruth McKoy Lowery

ROWMAN & LITTLEFIELD
Lanham • Boulder • New York • London

Published by Rowman & Littlefield
A wholly owned subsidiary of The Rowman & Littlefield Publishing Group, Inc.
4501 Forbes Boulevard, Suite 200, Lanham, Maryland 20706
www.rowman.com

Unit A, Whitacre Mews, 26-34 Stannary Street, London SE11 4AB

British Library Cataloguing in Publication Information Available

Library of Congress Cataloging-in-Publication Data

Names: Yenika-Agbaw, Vivian S., editor. | Hudock, Laura Anne, editor. |
  Lowery, Ruth McKoy, 1966– editor.
Title: Does nonfiction equate truth? : rethinking disciplinary boundaries
  through critical literacy / edited by Vivian Yenika-Agbaw, Laura Anne
  Hudock, and Ruth McKoy Lowery.
Description: Lanham, Maryland : Rowman & Littlefield, 2018. | Includes
  bibliographical references.
Identifiers: LCCN 2018004586 (print) | LCCN 2018006431 (ebook) | ISBN
  9781475842319 (Electronic) | ISBN 9781475842296 (cloth : alk. paper) |
  ISBN 9781475842302 (pbk. : alk. paper)
Subjects: LCSH: Language arts (Elementary) | Prose literature—Study and
  teaching (Elementary) | Interdisciplinary approach in education.
Classification: LCC LB1576 (ebook) | LCC LB1576 .D5865 2018 (print) | DDC
  372.6—dc23
LC record available at https://lccn.loc.gov/2018004586

For Joy, Luma, Yenik, again!—Vivian

To my parents, George & Frances, for their steadfast love and support—Laura

For my girls, Deandra, Que-My, and Tiffany—Ruth

Contents

Contents

List of Figures

List of Tables

Foreword

Building Our Capacity to Teach with Nonfiction

Kathy G. Short, University of Arizona, Director, Worlds of Words

This book on the possibilities of nonfiction texts in classrooms is particularly timely given the emphasis these texts are currently receiving within our broader society and in schools. At the global and national level, the Internet and social media are being used to churn out so much "fake news" that many people are no longer sure what news sources to trust. My local newspaper now runs a weekly section to debunk the most widely circulated false news stories of that week, providing evidence for why those stories are inaccurate.

At the school level, the Common Core Standards and their variations across states have brought a great deal of attention to nonfiction, calling for a 50/50 split between informational and literary texts starting in kindergarten, gradually increasing to a 70/30 split in high school. This emphasis on nonfiction is supported by research indicating that schools have focused almost exclusively on fiction in the past and not prepared students for reading the informational texts that fill their lives in college and careers.

This shift is also seen as important for engaging readers who prefer nonfiction for their own personal reading and who have often come to define themselves as nonreaders because of the emphasis on fiction in classrooms. Another indicator is research noting that only 10 to 15 percent of the texts read aloud by teachers in primary classrooms are nonfiction (Duke, 2000).

SHARING RESOURCES TO SUPPORT PROFESSIONAL LEARNING

The chapters in this book offer a range of resources for educators to support them in considering how they might engage children with nonfiction. Instead of providing formulas, the authors respectfully share resources along with underlying conceptual understandings so that educators can develop their own strategies for identifying texts and developing engagements around nonfiction in their classrooms.

They are given starting points to move ahead as professionals who take action in their classrooms, not just implement an expert's lesson plan. By building their knowledge base as teacher candidates and teachers, they create the foundation needed to make professional decisions related to the specific children and curriculum they encounter in classrooms.

One resource that many of the authors have integrated into their chapters is a discussion of terminology. Decisions about whether to call these texts nonfiction, informational books, or expository texts are based in the differing connotations and conceptual frames of each term. Even though the authors all value the role of these books with children, they have developed different terminology based on their experiences and expertise.

By providing space for each author to share their thinking about terminology instead of forcing everyone to use the same term, a better sense of the debates and complexities in the field is conveyed.

The authors of the chapters reject fiction and nonfiction as in opposition to each other. They challenge the common misconception that fiction consists of narrative text structures that tell a story, while informational texts use expository text structures to explain something. This distinction is overly simplistic as fiction and nonfiction both use narrative and expository writing and text structures.

Newkirk (2014) argues that informational text that engages readers always uses a narrative arc as the foundation because narrative is not a text type or genre but a mode of thinking used by nonfiction authors. The same is true of fiction where the story may be fictional but includes exposition because authors embed their own careful research and descriptions into stories.

Another resource included across chapters is discussions of what makes an effective high-quality nonfiction text. Each chapter author offers additional criteria and descriptions of these books and provides specific examples of titles to examine in order to develop deeper understandings of quality nonfiction. These titles provide a beginning point, but educators also need to understand the broader conceptual issues of why these titles are exemplary so they can select and evaluate nonfiction on their own to meet the needs of their students and the curriculum. In addition, the many websites and award lists provided in the chapters create a set of ongoing resources for educators to consult.

Often discussions of how to engage children with nonfiction do not go beyond teaching them how to use the special features found in these books, such as maps, diagrams, charts, and glossaries, or to identify the text structures for organizing information, such as sequence, comparison, and cause and effect. What is significant in these chapters is that the authors provide a range of engagements that emphasize how to encourage students to think critically about the ideas and information in these books.

These books are not just a source of facts for children's research but a place to critically consider and discuss different perspectives and broader societal issues. This view is a significant shift in thinking about the use of nonfiction in classrooms and puts a focus on inquiry and conceptual understanding, rather than fact-finding.

SHARING A VISION OF THE POSSIBLE IN CLASSROOMS

The authors of these chapters share a range of possibilities for bringing nonfiction into classrooms. This vision of the possible is not just listing a set of procedures but real examples of teachers sharing with each other about the ways nonfiction lives in their classroom settings.

Whenever authors take the position of sharing a classroom experience with other educators, they also invite readers to consider their experiences. As I read the chapters, my own experiences with nonfiction immediately leapt to mind, providing me with many connections and extensions. One connection from my own work is the need to balance the use of fiction and nonfiction within children's inquiries.

A fiction story provides a single point of view, one family or character, while nonfiction develops an understanding of the extent of an issue or problem in our world. Nonfiction provides definitions, terminology, and facts to make the issues real—not just an interesting story, but something that is actually occurring in the world. Through story, students understand the human emotions and struggles related to scientific or social issues, and, through nonfiction, they explore the broader world context of those issues.

I worked collaboratively with teachers to develop an inquiry about hunger in a local elementary school. We found students needed both stories and informational texts to understand this global issue (Thomas & Short, 2009). They needed to explore the extent of the problem of hunger, especially since most had not experienced hunger themselves.

Hunger affects many people in the world and the results are dire, going far beyond the stomach rumblings that students associated with being hungry. Characters in fiction usually found solutions to hunger that did not reflect the realities of ongoing chronic hunger. Informational texts helped students develop an understanding of the extent and severity of the problem and the lack of easy solutions, along with a recognition that the problem exists in their own community as well as around the world.

Fiction, however, was essential to humanize the numbers. Through story, students came to feel empathy and sympathy for those who go hungry, and through information about the extent and causes of the problem, they felt the need to get involved and be socially responsible. Story also kept them focused on larger social issues of power instead of getting lost in only gathering statistics on hunger without a broader conceptual frame within which to understand those issues.

This experience also provided constant demonstrations of the need to have multiple nonfiction texts in order to encourage students to compare information across texts. Our mantra became to never read a text alone and to always have other texts for comparison and discussion. These comparisons included a consideration of an author's perspective and positionality. Just as with fiction, we encouraged students to research the authors' backgrounds and experiences in relation to the content as well as their research strategies—to ask "how does this author know?" Most nonfiction authors provide extensive documentation on their websites of their processes in researching and writing a book along with author's notes in their books.

Because we wanted to signal to children that all literature, including nonfiction, should be considered critically, not accepted without question, the first questions we asked them to invite discussion after reading nonfiction were, "What are you thinking about? What connections did you make?" By starting with these questions, students were invited to share their interpretations and meaning-making around ideas based on current knowledge and experiences as well as to challenge those interpretations.

These discussions also helped develop a larger conceptual frame before moving to a focus on information. We then asked students to consider, "What was the text about?" and "What did you learn in this text?" to encourage them to cite evidence from within these texts and information to inform their inquiries. Finally, thinking about "How does this text work?" helped them explore the function of different nonfiction text structures and features in conveying information. This process allowed us to ground our work in reading as a transactional process (Rosenblatt, 1938) for nonfiction as well as fiction.

My experiences working with nonfiction in children's inquiries connect to the engagements and issues shared in these chapters. Other educators reading this book will also connect to experiences from their work in classrooms as well as gain new ideas. These classroom engagements provide a vision of the possible for teachers and again reflect the respect for teachers as professional learners that is evident across this book.

TEACHING AS CAPACITY-BUILDING

Many professional books about the use of nonfiction in classrooms are based in a reform mentality of forcing change to fix schools. Calls for reform often bring a negative response because these efforts typically revolve around a deficit view of teachers and schools. Reforms emphasize fixing what is wrong and attempt to force change through accountability, standards, and mandated programs.

In contrast, this book emphasizes building the capacity of teachers by positioning them as competent and knowledgeable and highlighting processes of professional learning that can develop their agency as decision makers. Teachers engage in building their knowledge base and therefore their capacity, not because something is wrong, but because teaching is an ongoing process of professional learning (Short, 2016).

This perspective on teaching is woven throughout this book, providing a valuable source of learning, rather than a formula for teachers to implement without deep understanding. Instead of defining change as fixing what is wrong, change is a stance of inquiry through which teachers explore new understandings about learning and literature. The need to bring more nonfiction into schools can either be viewed as an indicator of what is wrong with teachers and needs fixing, or as an opportunity for professional learning, the stance taken by these authors.

In capacity-building, teachers no longer work in isolation, but as members of a team, thinking alongside other educators to develop plans for change based on research, practice, and knowledge. In this case, they are invited to think alongside the educators who have written these chapters to share their experiences and knowledge about nonfiction.

REFERENCES

Duke, N. K. (2000). 3.6 minutes a day: The scarcity of informational texts in first grade. *Reading Research Quarterly, 35*(2), 202–225.

Newkirk, T. (2014). *Minds made for stories: How we really read and write informational and persuasive text.* Portsmouth, ME: Stenhouse.

Rosenblatt, L. (1938). *Literature as exploration.* Chicago: Modern Language Association.

Short, K. (2016). Advocacy as capacity-building. *Research in the Teaching of English, 50*(3), 349–364.

Thomas, L., & Short, K. (2009). Integrating fiction and nonfiction texts to build deep understanding. *WOW Stories, 1*(3). http://wowlit.org/on-line-publications/stories/storiesi3/7/.

Acknowledgments

This professional contribution would not have been possible without the support of our families, friends, colleagues, administrators, and the interlibrary loan staff at the Pennsylvania State University, who made sure we had access to the relevant professional resources in a timely manner. In addition, a special thank you goes to Tom Koerner, whose faith in the project and constant encouragement kept us focused, and to the Rowman & Littlefield production and editorial teams, especially Carlie Wall and Emily Tuttle for their guidance throughout the project.

We thank the reviewers whose constructive feedback helped to make this project a reality, and Kathy G. Short for agreeing to write the foreword. A book is nothing without the dedication of the authors; thus, we thank all the contributors who worked diligently on their chapters and responded in a timely manner to editorial reminders to bring this project to fruition.

We are thankful to the students whose writing samples and artifacts are included in this book, and wish that all their dreams come true. Additionally, we wish to thank Deborah Wooten, Keesha Jackson-Muir, and Adelle Sumner for agreeing to write blurbs for this book at short notice.

Introduction

Vivian Yenika-Agbaw

This book focuses on nonfiction texts (literary, nonliterary, informational) in various formats. Its primary purpose is to raise awareness to the abundant possibilities that such texts might offer to learners. The book stems out of several conversations with teacher candidates about nonfiction in our children's literature methods courses over the years. Teacher candidates who are passionate about children's literature often do not know how to situate nonfiction texts in their curriculum.

Hanging on to the basic notion of the genre as truthful, these teacher candidates are often uncertain as to how to approach nonfiction as literary texts that warrant careful and/or critical readings. They also struggle to integrate the texts in their curriculum in order to spawn multifaceted experiences that would nurture students as researchers and creators of meanings, while meeting national and/or state standards. Nonfiction texts also expand notions of literacy, enabling learners to inquire, discover, and act.

With this simple goal in mind, our book demonstrates that there is no mystery about nonfiction as a genre. Rather, it is malleable, and the literacy purposes of the educator and/or reader help to determine its role in the curriculum and in an individual's life. Thus, another major goal of this book is to introduce various critical approaches that might inform one's reading and analysis of nonfiction texts, and guide conversations and literacy events around specific texts selected for one's curriculum. This is based on the underlying principle of teacher candidates as teacher-scholars whose practices are informed by research.

Our expectation here is that readers of this book mediating children's experiences with nonfiction would cultivate the critical habits of mind that nudge us to carefully look at the words, drawings, pictures, and maps that contribute in bringing alive nonfiction narratives—how they are arranged and positioned on pages and between texts in order to discern what could be true about the facts presented on any topic. This may then lead to the beginnings of conversations that are thoughtful and critical.

Texts that utilize sound effects also demand this kind of careful scrutiny, since the sounds become signifiers that are employed to sway readers'/listeners' emotional, psychological, and cognitive engagements with the events and activities explored in such texts.

In the chapters that follow, contributors share how conversations unfold or might unfold around interesting topics in nonfiction texts: about art, language, math, science, and life in general in educational and other settings. They invite other educators new to the profession, for instance, teacher candidates, to also join in this "truth-seeking" and "truth-making" quest via nonfiction storytelling.

While contributors approach the project as potential mentors because of their years of experience, they are also mindful of the fact that *we are all learners*, and as such are still grappling with questions on how to create possibilities for *all child learners*. What they theorize about nonfiction (creative, literary, narrative, informational/expository), describe about instances of their practices, and share generally in their chapters in addition to how they design their inquiry to facilitate understanding of specific phenomena should serve as starting points for readers of this book.

OVERVIEW OF THIS BOOK

There are nine chapters altogether. Contributing to these chapters are schoolteachers, university professors and doctoral students who teach literacies, children's and adolescent literature, and a children's trade book author. They discuss how nonfiction is integrated in the school curriculum to facilitate learning in the content areas, learning of English language arts, and exciting ways such learning is fun-filled. Additionally, they contribute a wealth of researched ideas for classroom practice.

But most of all, they draw attention to the fact that nonfiction is not the opposite of fiction. Each chapter privileges inquiries, or ways of knowing specific to the investigative methods employed by the contributor. Chapter 1 explains in greater detail why we need books on nonfiction. Chapter 2 describes the processes involved in creating narrative nonfiction, as well as some key features in expository writing that authors of nonfiction include to facilitate readers' engagement and interaction with texts.

Chapter 3 offers ideas on how to integrate nonfiction in the curriculum to motivate learners to think critically. Chapter 4 highlights the importance of introducing nonfiction in an early childhood setting, noting that contrary to common practice, both the efferent and aesthetic stances are effective approaches to enhance information gathering and delight learners. Chapter 5 argues for the adoption of a critical visual literacy lens when approaching photographic images in nonfiction picture books.

Chapter 6 discusses findings of a study at a rural school district to illustrate the significant role that nonfiction plays in science learning, and expands the reader's understanding of what constitutes nonfiction texts. Chapter 7 explores how nonfiction might rekindle wonder, discovery, and curiosity among adolescents engaged in science literacies. Chapter 8 shares ideas about informational books that explore math concepts and discusses possible ways teachers might make nonfiction texts come alive in the classroom in order to stimulate more interest in mathematics through storytelling. Chapter 9 shares useful resources for educators to engage in critical conversations around nonfiction texts.

The chapters model aspects of "engaged pedagogy" (bell hooks, 1994) that prioritize relational learning between students, and among students and teachers, that centers community building through ongoing dialogue, and recognizes the art and acts of teaching and learning as attempts to hold fast to our humanity in its various manifestations. For hooks:

> Progressive, holistic education, "engaged pedagogy" is more demanding than conventional critical . . . pedagogy. For . . . it emphasizes wellbeing. That means that teachers must be actively committed to a process of self-actualization that promotes their own wellbeing if they are to teach in a manner that empowers students. (1994, p. 15)

The contributors strive to accomplish this, explaining their distinct approaches to text selection and student engagement with texts, and reflecting on multiple texts that ensue from such engagements. Through these engagements, we hope readers get a sense of how some educators approach nonfiction texts—literature and otherwise—in the K-16 classroom, noting practices that are informed by critical theories and sound pedagogy albeit from multiple perspectives.

REFERENCE

hooks, b. (1994). *Teaching to transgress: Education as the practice of freedom.* New York: Routledge.

Chapter One

Why Critical Conversations on Nonfiction Children's Texts?

Vivian Yenika-Agbaw

An immediate response to the title question is "Why not?" Growing up, my children often wondered what was true or false about Africa, the continent of their mother's national origin. On further reflections on their questions, the response remains the same: *it depends* on the genre, who is writing, the region, and subject of interest. Above all, it depends on the author's lens through which he/she chooses to investigate the continent and the purpose for writing about Africa, and for focusing on a particular region.

While this response never seemed to alleviate their concerns and doubts about the images with which they were constantly bombarded in print and other media, it reassured them that "truth" is always subjective. But then this raises the question of how educators also perceive notions of truths, and in particular, truths about our natural worlds and social history—sociocultural spaces constructed in literary and nonliterary texts—through words and images in various formats. How do we engage students in critical conversations around such "truths," especially those that are paraded in nonfiction literature for children and adolescents?

This question is crucial, and is continually on the minds of the more than one thousand teacher candidates who have taken a "methods" course with me over the years on the teaching of children's/young adult literature. Though excited about the possibilities that nonfiction affords, many of these students voiced concerns that revolve around the way "truths" about our natural and sociocultural worlds are presented, and the kinds of "truth" that dominate the texts they would like to share with students.

For some, apprehensions include how to navigate texts about geological sciences that are presented in unique formats, such as the Magic School Bus series; how to extend experiences with books about our natural world such as Patricia Lauber's (1993) *Volcano: The Eruption and Healing of Mount St. Helens*, which spotlights the volcanic eruption and its aftermath.

There are also anxieties on how to engage adolescent readers in critical discussions on books that navigate our dubious sociohistorical past, for instance, Aronson and Budho's (2010) *Sugar Changed the World: A Story of Magic, Spice, Slavery, Freedom, and Science*; and how to elicit multimodal and other types of responses from encounters with documentaries, such as *Poor Kids* on the social class situation in the United States. Some are uncertain as to how to introduce memoirs such as Margarita Engle's (2015) *Enchanted Air: Two Cultures, Two Wings, a Memoir*, which chronicles U.S. involvement in Cuba as part of global politics.

In general, teacher candidates interpret nonfiction as a genre of literature that tells the truth. However, when they encounter mixed genres like fictionalized biographies, they are easily thrown off—and frankly, initially, so was I in the early phase of my career. For shouldn't "nonfiction" connote "truth"? In the next section, I briefly theorize truth only as it is relevant to nonfiction.

Beyond that, this chapter does not delve into the larger philosophical arguments that have spanned centuries and continue to inspire new dialogues today among scholars. It attempts thus to address upfront notions of facts and objectivity that may impose limits on the pedagogical possibilities of nonfiction texts within educational settings, especially in an era where fact checking has been reduced to Googling.

THEORIZING "TRUTH"

The English philosopher Bertrand Russell (1912) theorizes truth in very interesting ways that are useful in this project. In his chapter "Truth and Falsehood," he posits that "truth consists in some form of correspondence between belief and fact" (p. 19), noting further that "we . . . seek a theory of truth which (1) allows truth to have an opposite, namely falsehood, (2) makes truth a property of beliefs, but (3) makes it a property wholly dependent upon the relation of the beliefs to outside things" (p. 20). Truth, thus, as presented in the first instance, could be seen in binary terms whereby learners may assume that if something is not a fact, then it is false.

However, taking into consideration how belief systems often inform daily practices and people's understanding of phenomena, truth then becomes subjective and relative and is shaped by other variables. The natural and scientific worlds (history) and social history are thus interpreted from these perspectives of subjectivities and relativity. In other words, as noted further in the *Stanford Encyclopedia of Philosophy* (2002–2015) by Marian David, a professor of philosophy:

> Members of the family employ various concepts for the relevant relation (correspondence, conformity, congruence, agreement, accordance, copying, picturing, signification, representation, reference, satisfaction) and/or various concepts for the relevant portion of reality (facts, states of affairs, conditions, situations, events, objects, sequences of objects, sets, priorities, tropes). (http://plato.stanford.edu/entries/truth-correspondence/)

There are other arguments for the existence of multiple truths or what some refer to as "truth pluralism" (Pederson & Wright, 2013). This first volume on nonfiction explores such forms of truth as represented in texts, performed through classroom practices, and negotiated or mediated through discussions with students within an environment of trust.

If we accept philosopher Paul Pardi's (2015) definition of truth as "a statement about the way the world actually is" (unpaged), we may then proceed with the following question: from whose perspective, and what motivates the specific version of truth? This is a strand of conversation that runs through some of the chapters across all three volumes in the series.

Pardi (2015) complicates our understanding of this concept further, discussing three major perspectives of truth held by some philosophers:

> The coherence theory describes truth in terms of interconnected belief. A belief is true if it is consistent with other beliefs we have. The correspondence theory describes truth in terms of a relation concepts or propositions have to the actual world. . . . [P]ostmodernism lays out a view of truth in terms of individual perspectives and community agreement. (unpaged)

From this brief summary, it is clear that truth is perceived variously depending on one's belief system. Thus, defining this concept can be quite exhausting. However, if a major quest of authors and artists who write and/or create nonfiction literature/texts is related to truth seeking, as insinuated by Aronson in his interview with Reading Rockets (http://www.readingrockets.org/books/interviews/aronson/transcript), how do we equip young readers with critical literacy skills that may enable them to investigate these "truths" in meaningful ways without becoming jaded?

How do we support them to cultivate critical mind-sets that may help to maximize the use of their creative imagination to afford them more opportunities to participate in truth seeking and truth making, as informed readers who engage in dialogue with texts, authors who create texts, and researchers who are committed to inquiry? How do we foster a culture and/or attitude of skepticism that may enable them to refrain from the culture of consumerism, which often predisposes us—*learners*—to accepting nonfiction contents as truths?

How do we also nurture them to perceive themselves as creators of meanings that are informed by belief systems steeped in human values and rigorous research? How might we mediate their literacy experiences, so they can think and act like the professional artists whose visual, verbal, and musical texts they have come to embrace as vehicles of truths? In several ways, this is a major thrust of the three volumes in this nonfiction series!

SHOULD DEFINITIONS MATTER?

They used to, but not as much now, as our understanding of nonfiction literature continues to shift. Georgia Heard (2013) captures this nicely, noting that "We can define fiction as being about imaginary events and people, and nonfiction is writing that deals with facts and gives us information and offers opinions. Both genres need to feel true" (p. 8). This is as simple as it can get. Although defining nonfiction poses a challenge to educators, we continue to ponder ways that we could present information about this subgenre that would make sense to students.

It is one thing for us adult learners and teachers to make the shift from our former understanding or assumptions of/about nonfiction as "not fake" (Beers & Probst, 2015, p. 21), to a novel awareness of nonfiction as dynamic and complex. This new realization is made more evident in Aronson and Zarnowski's (2015) claim that "Nonfiction is not 'true,' nor is it limited to facts, nor is its highest value being reliable." Rather, since "we live in an age of information glut[,] [o]ur students are a keystroke away from contrary evidence, new approaches, and dissenting views. Our job, then, is to prepare them to inquire, to research, and to think" (p. 20). This aligns with the goals of the book series.

Similar to these authors, contributors agree that placing inquiry at the center of genre study and text exploration affords learners with more possibilities to critically engage with nonfiction literature for children and adolescents. It enables them to have "conversation[s] with sources" (p. 28), which under the old paradigm they might have simply accepted as facts and worse yet, "truths."

In addition, the investigative process opens new opportunities for learners to experience nonfiction differently, departing from the consumption mindset that informs our curricular and secular practices and immersing them in what Aronson and Zarnowski (2015) posit as openings for adventures, and thus brings readers "one more step into the endless secrets, mysteries, and treasures of the universe" (p. 33).

Often too, we may be confused about the use of the terms *nonfiction* and *informational books*. In their 1992 book, *Using Nonfiction in the Elementary Classroom*, Freeman and Person debated the use of these terms and finally settled on using them "interchangeably to mean those books in the Dewey decimal classification that have numerical or biographical designation, with the exception of poetry and folklore" (p. vii). This chapter adopts this practice, bearing in mind the designation ascribed to books considered nonfiction by major awards in the field such as the Orbis Pictus and the Robert F. Sibert Medal. Both value factual accuracy and authentic writing, but exclude poetry and folktales from consideration.

In the opening chapter of Freeman and Person's (1992) *Using Nonfiction*, Russell Freedman discusses his views on this complex genre noting that

> Someone else has said that fiction is a pack of lies in pursuit of the truth. As a corollary, I suppose you could say that nonfiction is a pack of facts in pursuit of the truth. Unfortunately, facts can't always be trusted. Facts can be unreliable, misleading, ambiguous, or slippery. (p. 2)

He illustrates this point with examples from his own research as an author of nonfiction books, revealing to readers how the way people have been socialized in different communities and assaulted by media images can inadvertently lead to the documentation of misleading facts. As he notes, collecting data can be tricky, for there are always many points of view.

In the end, the author needs to make a decision about the "set of historical 'facts'" to privilege. Thus, "Just because the book is allegedly based on fact doesn't mean that it tells the truth" (p. 3). These are worthy nuggets to consider when sharing nonfiction books with children.

REFERENCES

Aronson, M., & Zarnowsky, M. (2015). Teaching nonfiction with confidence: Learning to love inquiry. In D. A. Wooten & B. Cullinan (Eds.), *Children's literature in the reading program: Engaging young readers in the twenty-first century* (pp. 20–34). 4th edition. Newark, DE: International Literacy Association.

Beers, K., & Probst, R. (2015). *Reading nonfiction: Notice and note, stances, signposts, and strategies*. Portsmouth, NH: Heinemann.

David, M. (2002–2015). The correspondent theory of truth. In *Stanford Encyclopedia of Philosophy*. Retrieved from http://plato.stanford.edu/entries/truth-correspondence/.

Freeman, E., & Person, G. (1992) (Eds.). *Using nonfiction trade books in the elementary classroom: From ants to zeppelini*. Urbana, IL: NCTE.

Frontline PBS. (2012). *Poor Kids.* Retrieved from http://www.pbs.org/wgbh/frontline/film/poor-kids. Produced by Jezza Neuman and Lauren Mucchiolo.

Heard, G. (2013). *Finding the heart of nonfiction: Teaching 7 essential craft tools with mentor texts.* Portsmouth, NH: Heinemann.

Pardi, P. (2015). What is truth? *Philosophy News.* Retrieved from http://www.philosophynews.com/post/2015/01/29/What-is-Truth.aspx.

Pederson, N., & Wright, C. (2013) (Eds.). *Truth and pluralism: Current debates.* Oxford University Press.

Russell, B. (1912). Chapter 1: Truth and falsehood. Retrieved from https://mitpress.mit.edu/sites/default/files/titles/content/9780262621458_sch_0001.pdf (pp. 17–24).

Transcript from an interview with Marc Aronson. Retrieved from (http://www.readingrockets.org/books/interviews/aronson/transcript).

CHILDREN'S BOOKS CITED

Aronson, M., & Budhos, M. (2010). *Sugar changed the world: A story of magic, spice, slavery, freedom, and science.* New York, NY: Clarion Books.

Engle, M. (2015). *Enchanted air: Two cultures, two wings, a memoir.* Illustrated by Edel Rodriguez. New York, NY: Simon & Schuster.

Lauber, P. (1993). *Volcano: The eruption and healing of Mount St. Helen's.* New York, NY: Simon & Schuster.

Chapter Two

Defining and Describing Expository Literature

Melissa Stewart and Terrell A. Young

At one time, nonfiction for children routinely included dry, stodgy expository writing—prose that explains, describes, or informs. Laden with text, these books had just a few scattered images that decorated, rather than enriched, the content and meaning. But nonfiction has changed dramatically over the last few decades, evolving in exciting new directions. Melissa entered publishing as a nonfiction editor for Franklin Watts in the early 1990s, and Terrell began teaching children's literature at the same time, so we've both witnessed the incredible metamorphosis from an insider's perspective.

Melissa has vivid memories of pasting up books. First, the illustrations and blocks of text were cut out with scissors. After slathering the backs of them with rubber cement, book pages were created by hand. Because the page-makeup process was tedious and labor intensive, changes were avoided at all costs, which stifled the creativity of the people whose job it was to lay out the books.

Fortunately, desktop publishing software transformed the way books are made. By the late 1990s, most of the world's major publishing companies had transitioned to the new technology. But the small, agile British publisher Dorling Kindersley was a decade ahead of its competitors. It was an early adopter of desktop publishing and quickly developed its innovative Eyewitness Books series.

Eyewitness Books became available in the United States in 1991, and within a few years, the beautifully designed, lavishly illustrated titles with short text blocks and extended captions had revolutionized children's nonfiction. These groundbreaking books gave fact-loving kids a fresh, engaging way to access information and spawned a massive category of nonfiction books now known by such names as "browseable books," "data books," and "factoid books."

Around the time that Eyewitness Books were catching on, a few children's authors began crafting narrative nonfiction—prose that tells a true story or conveys an experience. Some of the early standouts included *The Great Fire* by Jim Murphy (1995), *An Extraordinary Life* by Laurence Pringle (1997), and *The Snake Scientist* by Sy Montgomery (1999). This style of writing slowly gained momentum during the 2000s, and today, it's both incredibly popular and highly esteemed.

Narrative nonfiction appeals to fiction lovers because it includes real characters and settings; narrative scenes; and, ideally, a narrative arc with rising tension, a climax, and denouement. The scenes, which give readers a bird's-eye view of the world and people being described, are linked by expository bridges that provide necessary background while speeding through parts of the true story that don't require close inspection (Fleming, 2015). The art of crafting narrative nonfiction lies in selecting just the right scenes to flesh out.

The ratio of narrative text to expository text varies widely in narrative nonfiction (Colman, 2007). Most biographies are brimming with narrative scenes, while books that focus on historical events often include a bit more exposition. Science-themed books like *Neighborhood Sharks: Hunting with the Great Whites of California's Farallon Islands* by Katherine Roy (2014), *When Lunch Fights Back: Wickedly Clever Animal Defenses* by Rebecca L. Johnson (2014), and *Giant Squid* by Candace Fleming (2016) devote roughly equal numbers of pages to storytelling and explanations.

THE RISE OF EXPOSITORY LITERATURE

After the U.S. Congress passed the No Child Left Behind Act of 2001, school funding priorities suddenly shifted. School library budgets were slashed, and many school librarians lost their jobs. At the same time, a national economic recession threatened public library budgets too.

By the mid-2000s, the proliferation of websites made straightforward, kid-friendly information widely available without cost, which meant general survey books about lions or earthquakes or the Boston Tea Party were no longer mandatory purchases for libraries.

As nonfiction book sales to schools and libraries slumped, authors, illustrators, and publishers had to find new ways of creating books that would appeal to teachers, librarians, and the students they serve. The result was a new breed of visually dynamic, engaging expository literature that delights as well as informs.

WHAT *EXACTLY* IS EXPOSITORY LITERATURE?

According to the *Oxford English Dictionary* (n.d.), literature is "written works, especially those considered of superior or lasting artistic merit." And so we are defining expository literature as writing that explains, describes, or informs with "superior or lasting artistic merit."

Some leading literacy educators use the term *informational text* to describe nonfiction books that explain, describe, or inform (Aronson, 2016; Belfatti, 2015; Duke, 2000; Maloch & Bomer, 2013). But because the library community and Common Core State Standards define "informational book" and/or "informational text" differently (Belfatti, 2015; Maloch & Bomer, 2013; Stewart, 2016; Young & Ward, 2012), we prefer the term *expository text* for the sake of clarity.

We classify an expository nonfiction text as expository literature, if it (a) is meticulously researched and fully faithful to the facts, (b) features captivating art and dynamic design, and (c) incorporates a creative mix of the following text characteristics: strong voice, carefully chosen point of view, innovative text structure, purposeful text format, and rich, engaging language. This chapter describes each of these text traits in detail and explains how and why seven award-winning children's book authors focus on them as they craft their nonfiction manuscripts.

THE VOICE CHOICE

At one time, most editors rejected nonfiction manuscripts with a strong, distinct voice. They believed that the information conveyed, not the author's personality or perspective, should be the major attraction. But today, voice is recognized as an important element of engaging nonfiction.

Nonfiction voice options span a continuum, from lively to lyrical. For each manuscript, writers let their topic and their purpose for writing guide them to the best voice choice.

In *Pink Is for Blobfish: Discovering the World's Perfectly Pink Animals* (2016), author Jess Keating deftly employs a humorous, conversational voice, as shown in this excerpt (p. 3):

Pretty in Pink?
    The blobfish was recently voted the ugliest animal in the world in a poll taken by the Ugly Animal Preservation Society. Luckily, blobfish don't use mirrors, so they aren't bothered by their less-than-cute faces. As if this wasn't bad enough, another name for the blobfish is "fathead sculpin." These fish can't catch a break!

Keating chose this appealing, kid-friendly voice for *Pink Is for Blobfish* and its companion title *What Makes a Monster? Discovering the World's Scariest Creatures* (2017) because it allowed her to "dig into some fairly complex scientific concepts, while still keeping things approachable, funny, and memorable." When writing nonfiction, her goal "is never simply to provide the best information, but to do it in a way that gets the reader wanting to share it themselves with someone else." She believes that when books about science have a "light and approachable voice, readers aren't intimidated, and they're given the tools to carry on their own conversations about the topics in the book."

Dianna Hutts Aston says that the world fills her with awe, and the wondrous, soothing, lyrical voice of her nature writing reflects that. "I'm first an observer," she says, "so much makes me marvel and wonder. Just watching a squirrel work at getting to the meat of a pecan or a green snake tasting the air among purple pansies is poetry that I try to give words to. For me, it's a feeling of playing. Words are my toys."

Consider this passage from her book *A Butterfly Is Patient* (2011, p. 3):

A butterfly is patient.
It begins as an egg beneath an umbrella of leaves, protected from rain, hidden from creatures that might harm it . . . until the caterpillar inside chews free from its egg-casing, tiny, wingless, hungry to grow.

When Aston sat down to write this book, the voice was "simply there in my mind, not consciously considered." The text feels calm and soothing because, for her, "nature *is* soothing. In a world that often doesn't make any sense at all, the order of nature always does. Nature is the absence of confusion. It is a comfort."

EXPERIMENTING WITH POINT OF VIEW

Traditionally, expository nonfiction books for children featured a third-person point of view, but in recent years, authors have begun experimenting with other kinds of narration. Brenda Z. Guiberson credits her editor, Laura Godwin, for encouraging her to give first-person narration a try.

"For a long time, I had been looking for a simple and fun way to write about dinosaurs," Guiberson explains. "Bragging about certain body features popped into my head, and I considered first person. But I wasn't sure if the manuscript could get published that way, so I wrote it in third person. When I showed it to my editor, she said, 'Why don't you try this in first person?' So I did."

Both Guiberson and Godwin loved the result, and that dinosaur manuscript eventually became *The Greatest Dinosaur Ever* (2013). Here's an excerpt (pp. 4–5):

> I was the greatest. I was the tallest and the biggest herbivore. I had a long neck with the highest reach into the trees. The earth shook when I walked.
>
> I, SAUROPOSEIDON, (SORE-oh-po-SY-don) was the greatest dinosaur of them all!

Guiberson followed up *The Greatest Dinosaur Ever* with two titles that have a similar format and point of view: *The Most Amazing Creature in the Sea* (2015) and *The Deadliest Creature in the World* (2016). All three books feature animal narrators that talk about themselves, sharing facts and ideas in a way that appeals to young readers.

Second-person point of view has become even more popular in expository books because it's a powerful way to connect with children. When an author engages readers by addressing them with "you," children feel as if the writer is speaking directly to them. Second-person narration can be particularly effective when it's paired with a lively voice.

As you read the following excerpt from Sara Levine's *Bone by Bone: Comparing Animal Skeletons* (2013, pp. 5–6), notice how addressing readers with "you" helps to make the information more accessible:

> Can you imagine how you'd look if we added some bones to your spine?
> What if your vertebrae didn't stop at your rear end?
> What if they kept going?
> YOU'D HAVE A TAIL!
> Tails are made of vertebrae. Lots of animals have tails.
> They wag on happy dogs and sweep side to side to help alligators swim through the water.

Besides writing books for children, Levine is an assistant professor of biology at Wheelock College in Boston, Massachusetts. She says, "I wrote *Bone by Bone* based on how I teach bones and comparative anatomy to college students." In those classes, she starts off with a game of Simon Says, sprinkling in questions like, "What kind of animal would you be if you had just a skull, vertebrae, and ribs?" and "What if your finger bones grew down to your feet?"

"Questions like these make students think about how our bodies are similar to and different from those of other animals," says Levine. "They also make learning interactive, relevant, and fun." As she crafted her manuscript, Levine realized that, just like her college students, "Children enjoy being addressed directly and being active participants in responding to questions that make them think, especially about silly possibilities."

SEARCHING FOR STRUCTURE

Most traditional nonfiction books have a description text structure, and nearly all narrative nonfiction has a chronological sequence structure. But expository literature can have a variety of text structures, and choosing just the right one is a critical part of crafting a manuscript.

Caldecott honoree Steve Jenkins says, "The text structure for a book usually emerges as I'm doing research, making notes, and writing early drafts." But sometimes the perfect structure is obvious from the start.

"Never Smile at a Monkey: And 17 Other Important Things to Remember was inspired by that phrase popping into my head when I read that macaques sometimes react violently to a human smile (a display of teeth). From the beginning, I knew that I'd base the book on a series of similar admonitions (never clutch a cane toad, never cuddle a cub, never touch a tang)." Because Jenkins planned to discuss many different creatures, he knew immediately that he'd be writing a "list book," which has a compare-and-contrast text structure.

According to Brenda Z. Guiberson, "every topic can be approached in numerous different ways." Before writers can settle on a text structure, they must "figure out what they most want to say, and then pick the approach that says it best." She knew that *Feathered Dinosaurs* "would be a 'list book' from the very beginning," but "it took a long time, and several false starts," to find the right structure for *Earth: Feeling the Heat.*

"I was trying to say too much about a complicated global issue," Guiberson explains. "Finally I decided to stick with specific details and let the situations speak for themselves. Then it became a cause-and-effect book."

Melissa likes to compare searching for a text structure to shopping for a pair of pants. When we shop for pants, we usually know what purpose we want them to serve. Are they for playing sports? Relaxing around the house? Going to a fancy party? Keeping their purpose in mind allows us to eliminate some pants pretty quickly. We can also rule out pants if they're the wrong size or a color we don't like. But at a certain point, we have to try on a few pairs of pants to see how they fit.

The same is true for selecting a nonfiction text structure. When writers consider their purpose for writing, identify their audience, and decide exactly what they're most excited to share with readers, they can quickly eliminate some text structures. For example, a sequence structure won't work if the topic lacks a time element or natural order. Maybe there's no problem, and therefore no solution.

But like shopping for a pair of pants, at a certain point, a nonfiction writer often has to try on a couple of different text structures to see which one fits best. When Melissa was writing *Can an Aardvark Bark?* (2017), she experimented with four different text structures over a four-year period before finally deciding that a question-and-answer structure would work best.

WHY TEXT FORMAT MATTERS

Many high-quality expository titles, especially science-themed picture books, make skillful use of layered text, which consists of a short, simple primary text that conveys main ideas and secondary text that provides supporting details.

As you read books like *Mama Built a Little Nest* by Jennifer Ward (2014) and *An Egg Is Quiet* by Dianna Hutts Aston (2006), you will notice that the primary text, which is set in larger type to let children know that they should read it first, can stand on its own and provide a general overview of the topic. It also captures the imagination of young readers, inspiring them to continue reading.

In Jess Keating's *Pink Is for Blobfish* (2016) and *What Makes a Monster?* (2017), each double-page spread features four distinct layers, and each one has a different type treatment to guide young readers in navigating the pages.

On the left-hand page, readers see a headline paired with a photo that "grabs attention without overloading the reader." Main text at the top of the right-hand page introduces the animal and helps readers understand the creature's place in the world. A separate burst below the main text includes a tantalizing tidbit that "rewards the reader's interest." Keating says, "The main text and burst work in tandem, but the reader needn't read in a specific order to understand the information."

The final layer is a sidebar on the far right, where Keating lists details such as scientific names, habitats, and threats to the animals. This section is important to her because "some nonfiction readers zero in on figures and bullet points more easily than traditional prose. Being able to pick up simple, concrete information allows these readers to feel successful, which increases their engagement with the text."

Keating chose this multilayer approach to "give readers ownership over where they begin, and how long they stay on each page." Some children will "dive right in, get comfortable with the format, and never look up from a book until it's finished." Others may "dip their toes in first, not entirely sure if they want to continue."

With the recent popularity of graphic novels, authors are now experimenting with nonfiction in a graphic format. Many of these titles present information within the context of a storyline, but a few notable exceptions are entirely expository.

According to Steve Jenkins, when he and collaborator Robin Page began work on *How to Clean a Hippopotamus: A Look at Unusual Animal Partnerships* (2013), a book about animal symbiosis, "we realized that we'd need multiple illustrations to explain the back-and-forth nature of the creatures' relationships. The graphic novel format was intriguing from a design perspective, and it solved the problem of using multiple images to explain how animals interact. We also hoped that the graphic format's 'cool' factor might appeal to older readers."

Annette LeBlanc Cate, author-illustrator of *Look Up! Bird-Watching in Your Own Backyard* (2013), says that "the idea for using story panels and speech bubbles was there from the start. It felt very natural to me." And as Cate worked on the book, she realized that the format offered a number of advantages. "*Look Up!* was smallish book with a limited number of pages," she explains, "so there was only so much we could put in the running text." The graphic elements "really helped break up the text, and they provided a nice way to integrate all the other ways of presenting information—charts, observational tips, diagrams, charts. It was a great way to sneak in more stuff!"

The graphic elements in *Look Up!* also added a sense of lightheartedness that was important to Cate. "Unfortunately, bird-watching has a pretty stuffy reputation, and I wanted to write a book that kids would be excited to read. I really wanted to get kids engaged in not only the natural world, but their own personal inner one—the world of observing and drawing and keeping notes."

A LOOK AT LANGUAGE

Expository literature also differs from traditional expository nonfiction at the most basic level—word choice. Authors carefully select each and every word to craft text bursting with rich, powerful language that engages their young audience.

Consider the opening of *Rain, Rain, Rain Forest* by Brenda Z. Guiberson (2004, p. 3):

> Splitter, splat, splash! Rain gushes into the rain forest.
> It soaks the moss, drizzles off dangling vines, and thrums against slick waxy leaves.

The vibrant verbs in this passage paint a picture with words. They provide strong visual, auditory, tactile, and kinesthetic images that transport readers to the rain forest habitat and prepare them for an adventure.

Guiberson says that as she wrote this book, she packed it with "'rain words' to help the reader to see, hear, and feel the environment. Some of the vibrant verbs were in the first draft," she recalls. "But I went back several times and found more places to use them. I searched for quiet words, like 'has' or 'looks like' and replaced them with sloshing words that really thrummed and dripped with rain forest charm."

During the revision process, Guiberson sometimes uses a thesaurus to help her find the perfect word. She also reads her work aloud, listening to every syllable and sound, and asks other people to read it to her. "I pay close attention," she says. "Where do they hesitate or stumble? Where does the writing seem flat or quiet? What could be stronger? I go through this process several times."

As Melissa was writing *Feathers: Not Just for Flying* (2014), she relied on precise, vibrant verbs as well as similes to make the information more accessible. Here are some excerpts from the book's main text (pp. 3–7 and 22–23):

> Birds and feathers go together like trees and leaves, like stars and the sky.
>   Feathers can warm like a blanket . . . or cushion like a pillow.
>   Feathers can glide like a sled . . .
>   or sprint across the snow like snowshoes.

By comparing the surprising ways birds use their feathers to the way people use common, everyday objects, like blankets, pillows, sponges, and sleds, Melissa was able to make use of readers' prior knowledge to help them understand something new.

The excerpts also show how carefully chosen language devices can enrich expository writing. Because alliteration, opposition, and repetition infuse prose with phrases that are pleasing to the human auditory system, they can help writers craft a voice that is lovely and lyrical.

In *Frog Song* (2013), Brenda Z. Guiberson uses vibrant verbs, similes, alliteration, repetition, and onomatopoeia to enliven her text and highlight the incredible diversity of frogs and their mating calls. Here's an excerpt (p. 14):

> *In Spain*, the song of the male midwife toad clangs like a bell. TINK TINK TINK TINK! He carries a string of sticky eggs and crouches under a wet log to keep them moist. SQUIZZLE-SQUIZ. When he feels the tadpoles squirming, he hops, hops, hops to find a pool where they can hatch.

As Guiberson was crafting the text, she was already thinking about how the song sounds would look on the printed page. She requested setting the song sounds in different type because "people read words differently from the rest of the text if the type is falling down the page or vibrating at the edges." She hoped that drawing extra attention to these words would "inspire readers to sing, rather than read, the frog songs."

Combining language devices like puns, rhyme, alliteration, and surprising phrasing can make writing more humorous and playful, which is perfect for authors interested in crafting a lively voice. Consider these amusing headings from *Poison: Deadly Deeds, Perilous Professions, and Murderous Medicines* by Sarah Albee (2017):

Toxic Plots, Poison Pots, and Shipboard Shots
I Came, I Saw, I Poisoned
Heir Today, Gone Tomorrow
You Say Potato, I Say Be Careful

Albee includes this kind of language in *Poison* as well as *Bugged: How Insects Changed History* (2014) and *Poop Happened: A History of the World from the Bottom Up* (2010) to help middle-grade readers see just how "amazing and exciting and interesting history actually is."

"Sadly, kids are forced to read a lot of boring history textbooks," says Albee, "so my goal is to counteract those experiences." Simply put, she wants to "make books that are fun to read."

Albee notes that while her early drafts often include some lively writing, enriching her prose with "humor and energy is something I usually do at a late stage of revision. I carefully examine each sentence and think: How can I make this funnier, or more vivid, for my reader?"

To get her creative juices flowing, Albee often makes lists of words that relate to her topic. "Then I see if I can come up with alliterative adjectives." That strategy helped Albee think of the phrase "Deadly Deeds, Perilous Professions, and Murderous Medicines," which became the subtitle for *Poison.*

"I go to a rhyming website, such as rhymezone.com," Albee says "and find words that rhyme with one of the words on my list." She also hunts for "near rhymes" and synonyms that might be pertinent. "That's how I muscled out a header for *Poison* called 'No Bane, No Gain.'" When Albee was writing *Poop Happened*, she realized that *shovel* was a near rhyme to *chivalry*, "so I managed to come up with the heading 'The Age of Shovelry.'"

She also looks for ways to turn clichés or familiar phrases on their heads, such as Make New Friends, But Keep the Gold; Rest in Pieces; and Blood,

Sweat and Smears. "It can take a lot of mental energy to come up with a good turn of phrase," says Albee, "but it's so satisfying when I do!"

WHY STUDENTS NEED ACCESS TO HIGH-QUALITY EXPOSITORY TEXTS

Although the majority of adults who are passionate about children's literature are naturally drawn to stories and storytelling, many students are concrete, analytical thinkers who would rather read about data, facts, ideas, and information.

These budding scientists, engineers, mathematicians, computer programmers, accountants, electricians, and plumbers prefer expository literature with clear main ideas and supporting details. They're captivated by books that include patterns, analogies, concepts, diagrams, numbers, statistics, and calculations. As they read, their goal is to gather information so that they can learn about the world and how it works. They want to understand the past and the present, so that they can envision the future stretching out before them.

We strongly believe that the adults who make decisions about what books end up on classroom and library bookshelves aren't keeping the interests and needs of young analytical thinkers in mind. Educators need to honor these children by recognizing the key characteristics of expository literature and making it available to students.

But that's not the only reason to add a diverse array of expository literature to classroom and library book collections. Expository text is the style of nonfiction writing students will be required to produce most frequently in college and in their careers. Whether they're writing an essay or a dissertation, a business proposal, or a memo to their boss, they'll need the skills to summarize information and synthesize ideas so that they can craft prose that's clear, logical, and interesting. Finely crafted expository children's books are perfectly suited to serve as mentor texts for modeling these critical skills.

WAYS OF FINDING EXPOSITORY LITERATURE

Because many awards committee members have a natural preference for narrative writing, some prestigious awards consistently overlook exceptional expository titles (Stewart, 2015). This underrepresentation can make it difficult to identify expository books that should be added to classroom and school library bookshelves. Fortunately, the sources listed below generally include a good mix of notable narrative and expository nonfiction.

- AAAS/Subaru Prizes for Excellence in Science Books http://www .sbfonline.com/Subaru/Pages/PastWinners.aspx
- California Reading Association Eureka! Nonfiction Children's Book Award https://www.juniorlibraryguild.com/awards/view.dT/state-awards/ california/california-reading-association8217s-eureka-nonfiction -children8217s-book-awards
- Cook Prize for STEM Picture Book https://www.bankstreet.edu/center -childrens-literature/cook-prize/
- Cooperative Children's Book Center Choices List http://ccbc.education .wisc.edu/books/choices.asp
- Cybils Nonfiction Awards http://www.cybils.com/
- NCTE Orbis Pictus Award for Outstanding Nonfiction for Children http:// www.ncte.org/awards/orbispictus
- Nerdy Book Club Book Awards https://nerdybookclub.wordpress.com/

Two well-respected blogs showcase exceptional expository nonfiction as well as outstanding narrative nonfiction:

- Nonfiction Detectives www.nonfictiondetectives.com
- Nonfiction Picture Book Challenge, Wednesdays on Kidlit Frenzy http:// www.kidlitfrenzy.com

By using these resources as a guide, teachers and librarians can identify expository literature that will enrich and expand their collections.

REFERENCES

Aronson, M. (2016). The writer's page: What is narrative nonfiction? Retrieved from http://www.hbook.com/2016/03/choosing-books/horn-book-magazine/the-writers -page-what-is-narrative-nonfiction/.

Belfatti, M. (2015). Lessons from research on young children as readers of informational texts. *Language Arts, 92,* 270–277.

Colman, P. (2007). A new way to look at literature: A visual model for analyzing fiction and nonfiction texts. *Language Arts, 84,* 257–268.

Duke, N. (2000). 3.6 minutes per day: The scarcity of informational texts in first grade. *Reading Research Quarterly, 35,* 202–224.

Fleming, C. (2015). Ten secrets of writing narrative nonfiction. Presentation at the Society of Children's Book Writers and Illustrators Annual Summer Conference, Los Angeles, CA.

Maloch, B., & Bomer, R. (2013). Teaching about and with informational texts: What does the research say? *Language Arts, 90*(6), 441–450.

Oxford English Dictionary. (n.d.). http://www.oxforddictionaries.com/us/definition/american_english/literature.

Stewart, M. (December 2015). Diversity in thinking. A Fuse #8 production/*School Library Journal.* Retrieved from http://blogs.slj.com/afuse8production/2015/12/21/guest-post-melissa-stewart-and-diversity-in-thinking/#_.

Stewart, M. (Fall 2016). What the heck is an informational book? *The SCBWI Bulletin*, pp. 21–22.

Young, T. A., & Ward, B. A. (2012) Learning science content and skills: Informational text within the common core. *Book Links, 22*(3), 30–35.

CHILDREN'S BOOKS CITED

Albee, S. (2010). *Poop happened: A history of the world from the bottom up.* New York, NY: Bloomsbury.

Albee, S. (2014). *Bugged: How insects changed history.* New York, NY: Bloomsbury.

Albee, S. (2017). *Poison: Deadly deeds, perilous professions, and murderous medicines.* New York, NY: Crown.

Aston, D. H. (2006). *An egg is quiet.* San Francisco, CA: Chronicle.

Aston, D. H. (2011). *A butterfly is patient.* San Francisco, CA: Chronicle.

Cate, A. L. (2013). *Look up! Bird-watching in your own backyard.* Somerville, MA: Candlewick.

Fleming, C. (2016). *Giant squid.* New York, NY: Roaring Brook.

Guiberson, B. (2004). *Rain, rain, rain forest.* New York, NY: Holt.

Guiberson, B. (2010). *Earth: Feeling the heat.* New York, NY: Holt.

Guiberson, B. (2013). *Frog song.* New York, NY: Holt.

Guiberson, B. (2013). *The greatest dinosaur ever.* New York, NY: Holt.

Guiberson, B. (2015). *The most amazing creature in the sea.* New York, NY: Holt.

Guiberson, B. (2016). *The deadliest creature in the world.* New York, NY: Holt.

Guiberson, B. (2016). *Feathered dinosaurs.* New York, NY: Holt.

Jenkins, S. (2014). *Never smile at a monkey: And 17 other important things to remember.* Boston, MA: Houghton Mifflin.

Jenkins, S., & Page, R. (2013). *How to clean a hippopotamus: A look at unusual animal partnerships.* Boston, MA: Houghton Mifflin.

Johnson, R. (2014). *When lunch fights back: Wickedly clever animal defenses.* Minneapolis, MN: Millbrook.

Keating, J. (2016). *Pink is for blobfish: Discovering the world's perfectly pink animals.* New York, NY: Knopf.

Keating, J. (2017). *What makes a monster? Discovering the world's scariest creatures*. New York, NY: Knopf.

Levine, S. (2013). *Bone by bone: Comparing animal skeletons*. Minneapolis, MN: Millbrook Press.

Montgomery, S. (1999). *The snake scientist*. New York, NY: Houghton Mifflin Harcourt.

Murphy, J. (1995). *The great fire*. New York, NY: Scholastic.

Pringle, L. (1997). *An extraordinary life*. New York, NY: Orchard.

Roy, K. (2014). *Neighborhood sharks: Hunting with the great whites of California's Farallon Islands*. San Francisco, CA: Chronicle.

Stewart, M. (2014). *Feathers: Not just for flying*. Watertown, MA: Charlesbridge.

Stewart, M. (2017). *Can an aardvark bark?* New York, NY: Simon & Schuster.

Ward, J. (2014). *Mama built a little nest*. New York, NY: Simon & Schuster.

PERSONAL COMMUNICATIONS

Albee, S., March 9, 2017.
Aston, D. H., March 7, 2017.
Cate, A. L., March 15, 2017.
Guiberson, B., March 13, 2017.
Jenkins, S., March 15, 2017.
Keating, J., March 13, 2017.
Levine, S., March 7, 2017.

Chapter Three

Using Nonfiction to Motivate Students

Classroom Engagement

Elizabeth Raff

Today, teachers are constantly in battle with a world of distractions and expectations on our students. School can easily become a mundane place, where everyone becomes immune to the daily routine. However, where is the joy in learning? Where is the excitement and passion? Teaching nonfiction can be a wonderful opportunity to engage students in a new world. It can be a challenging experience, but when put in the right context, it can yield high results.

When teachers provide an uncommon experience for students, they will be rewarded with an uncommon effort and attitude (Burgess, 2012). That is the key to student engagement.

When rigorous curricular content and high-level engagement occur, students flourish. Active engagement requires them to be fully immersed in the lesson activities and process, motivating students to dig deeper into nonfiction texts because they are invested and challenged. These strategies, most of which come from my classroom practice, include text mapping, competition, using music and movement to reinforce nonfiction skills, room transformations, and utilizing current events to spark culturally relevant debate in the classroom. Creating an active learning environment is key to engaging students in complex nonfiction texts.

TEXT MAPPING

I have taught sixth grade for several years at a school district in Lancaster, Pennsylvania. For many of my students, nonfiction comprehension can be more challenging than fiction. Information told in story form becomes a more comfortable context because nonfiction texts require students to be more cognitively prepared. Text mapping is an excellent tool to bring nonfiction texts to life in a hands-on way. It is a graphic organizer technique where students see a nonfiction text as an entire scroll, not as individual pages in a textbook (Middlebrook, 2007).

Nonfiction texts are filled with much more than the words on a page, and this can be overwhelming for students. Text mapping allows students to take their time, observe all items, and focus on a specific skill at hand. When students view the entire text, they notice patterns, heading structure, illustrations, captions, and keywords. This activity can be used to teach a specific skill or work on comprehensive annotating skills that can be transferred to new texts students will come across. They can also identify how a specific text feature contributes to print comprehension.

After all text pages are copied and assembled with tape similar to a scroll, students work in small groups to observe what they notice, and specifically, what patterns they see. Choosing a specific color for headings, students box each heading and discuss what they predict this section will be about. Next, students select colors to box or circle illustrations, captions, and any other major text features that recur throughout the scroll. Choosing consistent colors for each feature allows students to see the structure of the text from a bird's-eye view.

Once all major text features are accounted for, the teacher models what students might annotate and text map in each written section. If there is a specific skill such as main idea and details, students color-code based on that skill. However, students can always annotate (circle, box, underline) for keywords, challenging vocabulary, names, places, and anything that is specific to the topic of the text.

It is essential that this is not the only reading of the text, just a preliminary one. In order for higher-level comprehension to take place, this quick annotating read has the sole purpose of annotating or working through the focus skill. After the entire text is mapped, students go back to reread the text with a higher level of understanding. Depending on the grade level and the length of the text, the second read can be done in sections instead of waiting until the entire text is mapped.

When students work collaboratively on text mapping, they become strategic and active readers, hearing what others observe and adding to the discussion. By starting with a bird's-eye view of the entire text, students notice relationships between text structure, text organization, and the meaning behind it. This hands-on activity is especially beneficial for students with learning disabilities because they physically section off areas of the text with a color-coding system. Most important, the text map becomes a visual record of a student's thought process. Text mapping allows students to be actively engaged in the reading process.

COMPETITION

Active games in the classroom are great ways to engage students in hands-on activities because motivation increases when competition drives a lesson. However, teachers walk a fine line between creating meaningful learning opportunities and wasting time for something that is just "fun." When games are brought into the classroom, it is essential that every student is held accountable for their learning and their own mental workload.

For example, *Jeopardy!*® in small groups is a common game structure used in any grade level and any subject. However, it is the smartest students in the group who typically answer the questions, and the rest of their classmates relax for the next twenty minutes because they feel they do not have much to contribute. This lack of accountability about games in the classroom can be problematic. When we introduce competition during a lesson, it must benefit all students involved by creating an active learning environment where every student is required to share the cognitive load.

In addition, these games should also stretch students beyond mere recall of information to embrace higher-level thinking skills such as those found in Bloom's taxonomy of learning (Armstrong, 2017). Introducing games that foster higher-level thinking such as comparing and contrasting, creating original examples, and synthesizing information is beneficial. When students are given an engaging activity while being challenged cognitively, they will flourish.

Scavenger Hunt

One foundational game for nonfiction learning that promotes active participation is a scavenger hunt of text features. Teachers can borrow copies of nonfiction texts from their school or local library that have a wide and diverse array of topics. Through this process, students are identifying the text features that they see in the texts but are also exposed to new texts they might want to check out in the future. This scavenger hunt can be flexible depending on grade level, curricula objective, and students' needs.

Lower elementary students might have a simple checklist they need to cross off when they see certain text features. In older grades, they can go through a similar checklist but then have to elaborate how that specific text feature enhances the understanding of the text or why the author chose to place it in that particular area. Students can work in pair competition by seeing how many features they can find of their specific text compared to their partner in a set amount of time. Once the timer goes off, they can rotate texts around the room so all students receive a variety of texts to apply their identification skill.

This specific structure can be morphed to the needs and accessibility of certain classrooms. For example, instead of staying in the classroom, teachers can place these texts around the school where students walk around to find the text and then complete the activity on their own. Additionally, if technology or personal devices are available, students can take pictures or small videos of the text features that they find and share them with their classmates. This makes the activity more culturally relevant for our technologically rich learners.

Jenga

Another game that works well with nonfiction texts is Jenga®. This is an engaging game where players take a wooden block out of a tower and place it on the top without letting the tower fall down. It has become a staple in many active classrooms because it can be applied to any grade level and any subject (King, 2015a). Students love the tension that Jenga creates, and they work carefully to ensure their tower does not fall down. This game can be used for skill application or review with task cards, questions posed on the front board, or scenarios that students have in front of them. For nonfiction lessons, this game can be used for identifying main idea and details, text features, or text structure.

Oh, Ick! 114 Science Experiments Guaranteed to Gross You Out! (Masoff, 2016) is a nonfiction text used with this game, which captivates some sixth grade students. Teachers can choose a section that either features a wide variety of text features or a specific experiment that elaborates with background information depending on the skill that is being reinforced. Once students are familiar with the section with a quick read, questions can be posted on the board or pretyped at their seats.

If using the game for main idea and details, students would view a small paragraph and have various questions about identifying the main idea and identifying three details from the text. They could also have questions that ask them to create a heading or subheading based on the paragraph, find a detail that does not support the main idea, or compare and contrast the details of two different paragraphs.

Students are placed in small groups with a Jenga set for each group. Everyone in the group answers the question individually and records their answer on a private paper or whiteboard. Once the correct answer is revealed, students compare how many people got it right or wrong in their group. If everyone in the group has the answer correct, they only have to move one block of that particular color up. If someone in the group has an incorrect answer, they have to move two blocks of that particular color.

To make the competition more intense, teachers can use various colored markers or paints to color-code the blocks involved in a Jenga set. For more on this check out the following blog: http://elizabethraff.com/2016/09/02/jenga-in-the-classroom/. Instead of letting students choose any block to move to the top, teachers can call out a particular colored block to move to further the game with more tension and competition.

A key to this game for engaging students in a constant flow of cognitive work is that there are no outs. Many times, in classroom games, once a group or a student is out, they do not have to do any more work. However, it is important for students to be constantly engaged in the learning process. Therefore, if a Jenga tower falls down, that group builds it back up and keeps working on the next question. You can record how many times the tower falls to decide the final winner at the conclusion of the questions.

Headbandz

Another game, that proves to be a hit among some sixth grade students is Headbandz™. This spin on flash cards has proven to be a crowd pleaser because they look goofy while doing it. Students need a stretchy headband over their forehead and a stack of cards. While working with partners, a word or phrase is attached on the front of someone's head. Their partner must describe or explain the word. When it is guessed, the student takes the card out of their headband and swaps it for a new one to continue the same routine.

This game requires both students to share the cognitive workload because one person needs to describe the word or phrase without any notes and the other must successfully identify what their partner is describing. Additionally, this game can be used for any type of vocabulary or skill and be moved up Bloom's taxonomy of learning (Armstrong, 2017).

For example, if the skill was identifying structures in a particular nonfiction text, the cards behind the headband would read: description, compare and contrast, chronological order, cause and effect, and problem and solution. In the first round, partners can use recall to explain the definition of each text structure. In the second round, partners can identify and explain the keywords associated with each structure. In the last round, partners can create an example to showcase that text structure.

A great nonfiction text to use with this game is *Story of the Titanic* (Noon, 2012) because there are multiple text structures woven throughout. It is essential that students do not view text structure as separate entities since many authors change text structure in the middle of a book depending on the topic. This text captivates students' interests and plays between chronological order, description, and cause and effect structures.

In the first and second round of Headbandz, students should simply review structures and keywords to jog their memory. In the third round, students should find an example in *Story of the Titanic* that showcases the structure their partner needs to guess. Both students are sharing this cognitive load because one student needs to search for an example of that text structure within a complicated text and the other needs to be prepared to identify it. This is a great way to join an engaging game while also promoting higher-level thinking skills.

MUSIC AND MOVEMENT

An active learning environment allows opportunities for students to use creativity to express themselves while reinforcing the main learning objectives. Using movement and music in the classroom is a great way to ensure students are becoming part of the learning process. Playing songs or raps to cover specific content or skills creates a positive learning environment and allows for quick retrieval for auditory or visual learners.

Music

When teaching the skill of main idea and details in nonfiction texts, students can follow a short rap that highlights the protocol or method for identifying this skill in a paragraph. This catchy and culturally relevant exercise can be reinforced at the beginning or end of a lesson for a few days to hook students. Flocabulary (2016) is a web resource that many educators rely on because it provides exciting, high content related raps and songs for grades K-12. These short videos are engaging and allow students to participate in the song process. They can dance on their chair to the rap, create motions that match the lyrics, and sing or rap along.

Some educators are also creating their own raps or songs for their students so that high-level vocabulary and specific skill reinforcers are brought to life. For example, Bethany Humphrey, a fourth grade teacher in Nevada, wanted to introduce the skill of nonfiction text structure to her students. She rewrote the lyrics to a famous song, "Ice Ice Baby," and titled it "Text Structure Baby" (Humphrey, 2016).

This engaging rap is packed with essential information that her students love to perform. It is the perfect hook at the beginning of a lesson to activate students' prior knowledge and get them ready to identify text structure. Furthermore, it gives students the opportunity to create their own raps or songs promoting a synthesis of information (Armstrong, 2017). This challenge is perfect for an end-of-unit project or assessment.

Movement

In addition to music in the classroom, movement can create an engaging environment and aid kinesthetic learners. Many educators use motions to help their students remember content-specific vocabulary words, skills, or steps to a process. Whole Brain Teaching is a popular method used in classrooms that activates movement to introduce or reinforce skills (Biffle, 2013). The main principles of a Whole Brain Teaching routine include the teacher and a group of students sitting in pairs.

The teacher explains information in small chunks, using motions to reinforce certain aspects of that information. For example, if the teacher is introducing nonfiction text features for *Story of the Titanic* (Noon, 2012), they will create a motion to symbolize each feature. Afterward, students reteach that information to their partner.

Signal words are used in this routine to create a fast-paced and engaging environment. At the beginning, the teacher will hold their hands up and say "mirrors." Students mimic this motion and verbally respond with "mirrors." Anything that is done when the mirrors are on is repeated by students. Afterward, the teacher uses a clapping motion to signal students to teach their partner. Teachers also use a signal "class, class" to end the teaching session.

It is important that this routine remains student centered. After the first day of modeling, the "teacher" should be a student in subsequent days. Also, instead of simply regurgitating information during the paired teaching moment, students should be required to either give examples of what they are explaining, elaborate on the topic, or engage in questioning that requires higher-level thinking. The Whole Brain Teaching routine is flexible and allows for teachers to make it work for their group of students, adding motions that are appropriate for their particular grade level.

ROOM TRANSFORMATIONS

Imagine being a student and walking into a typical classroom on any given day. The routine, the layout, and the expectations are all the same. Now, imagine coming to school one day to discover your classroom has been completely transformed into a new world. You would want to know what was happening and you would want to get involved. Room transformations are a great way to set the stage to engage students while challenging them in high content related activities.

By creating a new environment in the classroom, students become hooked because they do not feel that they are entering a classroom; they are entering an adventure. When creating a room transformation, it is essential that teachers do not become too focused on the pizzazz of the environment and forget the importance of the activity students will be completing. It is important that students are given a challenge that includes an immense amount of cognitive work because they are already motivated by the environment. If the room is transformed and students are not being pushed academically, the purpose of the transformation falls short.

For example, if a teacher is working on summarizing nonfiction texts with their students, creating a "spy lab" is a perfect choice for an engaging classroom transformation (King, 2015b). All you need is white string and black lights to create a laser beam effect in the classroom. Add some *Mission: Impossible* music in the background and your students will feel that they traveled to a secret CIA spy lab.

Students can read the text *The Dark Game* (Janeczko, 2010), which is a higher-level nonfiction text that requires focused reading. In folders, students can be told that the U.S. spy files have been hacked and they must read and annotate this text to recreate certain spy profiles for the U.S. government. They must summarize the most important pieces of text to include in the profile. This is a great challenge scenario that students will love to engage in. The room is transformed and the academic challenge is high.

There are also low-prep ways to create room transformations to catch students' attention. Lights are a great way to set the tone for a lesson. Flashlights or twinkle lights can be used for a camping scenario. Props to reinforce a nonfiction text can be placed around the room. Also, creating unique scenarios allows students to use their imagination. If teachers sell it with enthusiasm, students will love being in their classroom for a new purpose.

CURRENT EVENTS

When teachers use texts that are outdated, not culturally relevant, and do not provide an interest or spark, students become disengaged. However, using current-event articles is a great way to engage students in a topic that is relevant, intriguing, and provides the perfect landscape for nonfiction skill practice. There are many current-event web resources available to teachers, but two that are used widely by educators are Newsela and Time for Kids.

These resources provide current nonfiction articles that are intended for younger audiences. Specifically, Newsela (2017) provides all of their articles in multiple lexile levels so that teachers can differentiate their classroom and use articles that best fit their individual learners' needs. Most of the articles are also paired with a question set that focuses on comprehension and higher-level skills.

Current-event articles can be utilized for a wide variety of purposes. For example, they can be used to text map or annotate, make connections, and apply skills such as main idea and details, text structure, or creating inferences. These articles can be used as a hook at the beginning of the lesson, as direct instruction or modeling, small-group practice, or final assessment pieces.

A great activity that engages all students with these articles is a current-event debate. Once students are familiar with the topic and show their understanding, posing a controversial or engaging question to students can spark a dynamic discussion in the classroom. They should support their claims by using evidence in the article. The format can be flexible in small groups or whole group. I often assign a specific argument side to students to allow for higher-level thinking.

Finally, current-event articles are great tools to provide background knowledge or connect to other texts across content areas. They can be used to show students the relevancy of a topic. For example, if students are reading *A Long Walk to Water* (Park, 2010) about the lost boys of Sudan and refugee camps, teachers might encourage them to make connections to more recent events in the news. Students can read and annotate a current-event article about the Syrian refugee crisis, and make connections between the texts. Current-event articles provide a diverse array of purposes and support learners in their nonfiction journey.

CONCLUSION

It is clear that teachers must create a positive learning environment that engages students in the learning process. Nonfiction skills can be a challenge for many students, and educators must reflect on how they are engaging students and providing them with opportunities to be challenged. By setting the stage to engage, students are more likely to welcome that challenge.

Classroom-tested strategies that increase student engagement and provide rigorous activities include text mapping, competition, using music and movement to reinforce nonfiction skills, room transformations, and utilizing current events to spark culturally relevant debate in the classroom. Teachers set the tone for engagement in the classroom. If they showcase excitement and enthusiasm for a topic or activity, students will follow. Enthusiasm is contagious, and it is essential that educators step outside of the box to teach nonfiction skill so students can grow.

REFERENCES

Armstrong, P. (2017). Bloom's taxonomy. In Vanderbilt University Center for Teaching. Retrieved from https://cft.vanderbilt.edu/guides-sub-pages/blooms-taxonomy.

Biffle, C. (2013). *Whole brain teaching for challenging kids*. N.p.: Whole Brain Teaching LLC.

Burgess, D. (2012). *Teach like a pirate*. San Diego, CA: Dave Burgess Consulting, Inc.

Humphrey, B. (2016). Text structure. In *Teaching and so fourth*. Retrieved from http://teachingandsofourth.blogspot.com/2016/10/text-structure.html.

In *Flocabulary—Educational hip-hop*. (2016). Retrieved from https://www.flocabulary.com/.

In *Newsela—Instructional content platform*. (2017). Retrieved from https://newsela.com/.

In *Time for kids*. (2017). Retrieved from http://www.timeforkids.com/.

King, H. (2015a). Giant Jenga: Set the stage to engage. In *Elementary shenanigans*. Retrieved from http://www.elementaryshenanigans.com/2015/08/giant-jenga.html.

King, H. (2015b). Spy headquarters: creating engaging learning environments. In *Elementary shenanigans*. Retrieved from http://www.elementaryshenanigans.com/2015/06/spy-headquarters-creating-engaging.html.

Middlebrook, D. (2007). Improving reading comprehension skills instruction. In *The textmapping project*. Retrieved from http://www.textmapping.org/overview.html.

CHILDREN'S BOOKS CITED

Janeczko, P. B. (2010). *The dark game: True spy stories*. Somerville, MA: Candlewick Press.

Masoff, J. (2016). *Oh, ick! 114 science experiments guaranteed to gross you out!* New York, NY: Workman Publishing.

Noon, S. (2012). *Story of the Titanic*. New York: NY: Dorling Kindersley Limited.

Park, L. S. (2010). *A long walk to water*. New York, NY: Clarion Books.

Chapter Four

Teaching Young Readers Using Nonfiction Texts

Xenia Hadjioannou and Nancy Rankie Shelton

Traditionally, when thinking about literature for early childhood education, fictional narratives in the form of traditional and modern fairytales with princesses and talking animals or realistic tales of young children trying to figure out how they fit in the world come to mind. However, as Newkirk (1989) contends, even the youngest children are very interested in nonfiction, both in the texts they produce and the texts they read. Indeed, children's earliest compositions are often expository in nature and involve an effort to represent knowledge about the world and their place in it.

Frequent subjects include "my family," "my house," "my friends," as well as any other topic each young writer finds interesting and knows a lot about; from the weather, to different kinds of dinosaurs, to how germs make you sick (see figures 4.1 and 4.2). Children's questions about topics they find fascinating can lead to intense engagement with books on those very topics, often leading to multiple readings and to memorizing every word in the written text and every nuance in illustration.

Given young children's affinity for nonfiction, recent initiatives to bring more nonfiction texts into the younger grades have the potential to be powerful in igniting students' interest, fueling their learning, and helping them build comprehension strategies and reading stamina by maintaining deep engagement for extended periods of time. However, this potential can be dulled or even backfire if nonfiction texts are brought in the younger grades as recipes to be mastered instead of as complex texts to be enjoyed, mulled over, questioned, discussed with others, and evaluated.

In this effort, we must make a point to honor students' interests and background knowledge, to make available to them many high-quality nonfiction texts as part of a rich library collection of various genres, and to make time to have deep, critical conversations about the texts we read.

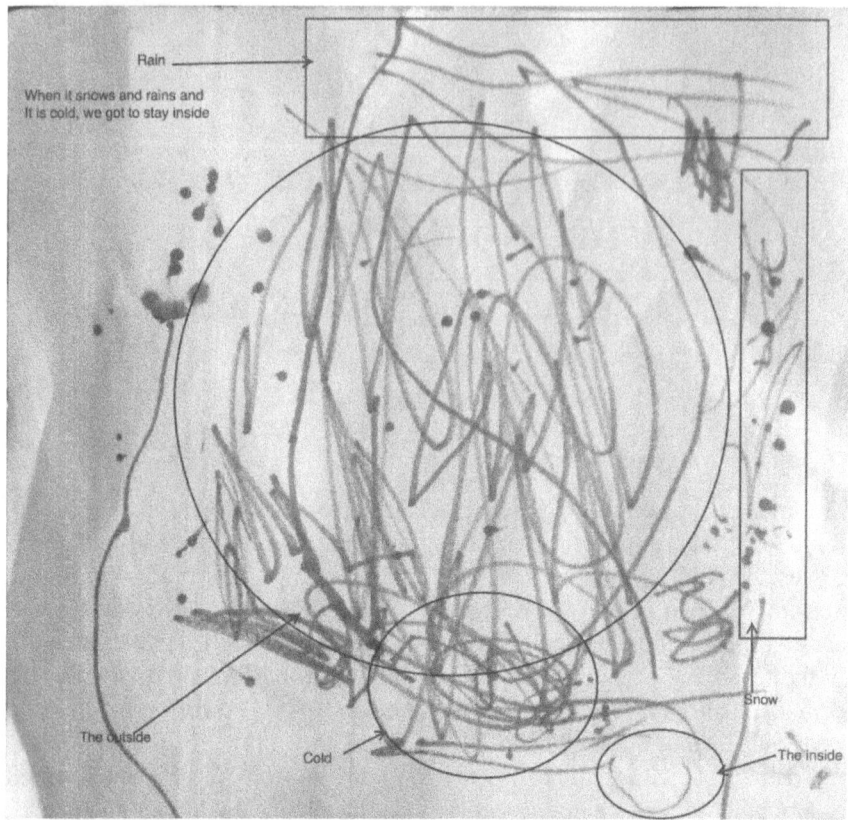

Figure 4.1. "Cold Weather" by Erik (2y, 6m), annotated with comments he made while drawing. *Source*: Xenia Hadjioannou.

Often, when talking about nonfiction texts, teachers assume that they must be read for efferent (Rosenblatt, 1995) reasons, forgetting that many exemplary nonfiction texts are structured in ways that are artistically compelling. It's important to realize that many nonfiction books can and should be read for aesthetic purposes before they are treated as texts to teach content information to young children.

School curricula typically guide pedagogical materials and decisions; however, these mandates often allow some flexibility in adding supplemental materials to meet standards as well as leeway in providing for the instructional decision making of teachers. *Swan: The Life and Dance of Anna Pavlova* (Laurel Snyder, ill. by Julie Morstad, 2015), *The Boy Who Loved Math: The Improbable Life of Paul Erdos* (Deborah Heiligman, ill. by LeUyen Pham, 2013), and *Brave Girl: Clara and the Shirtwaist Makers' Strike of 1909* (Michelle Markel, ill. by Melissa Sweet, 2013) are biographies, but these

Figure 4.2. "Spreading germs while coughing" by Erik
(6y, 11m). *Source*: Xenia Hadjioannou.

award-winning books are also beautiful stories of unknown heroes, people who contributed significantly to their communities.

These books can easily be used to teach or reinforce proficiencies such as recalling main idea and details, comprehension proficiencies such as comparing characters' attributes and their experiences, as well as examining the integration of knowledge presented in the texts and the illustrations. But the learning does not need to stop there. Critical analysis of the texts and the experiences they describe can include how each of these books, which begin during the hero's childhood, emphasize to the reader that overcoming obstacles (poverty, eccentric personality, and child labor exploitation, respectively) is possible and can lead to successful, exciting lives.

These texts are also global, with settings that begin in three different countries (Russia, Hungary, and the United States), emphasizing that human rights and equal opportunity are not restricted to a single country or society. In addition, such biographies welcome the exploration of a variety of critical issues such as evolving social norms and expectations (with an eye to issues of equity and social justice); the interrogation of the assumptions and values visible through the writing; and the consideration of the tension between historical fact and telling a vibrant, compelling story inherent in biography writing.

Children's curiosity, rather than curriculum, can also be the impetus for turning to nonfiction texts. When Erik, Xenia's[1] son, was five and in kindergarten, he was fascinated by the fact that invisible bacteria and viruses are what makes people sick. Xenia and Erik's father, Michael, read picture books about it, and thanks to YouTube, Xenia dug up some cartoons from her own childhood on this topic.

To further satiate Erik's growing interest in bacteria and viruses, Michael brought out the big guns: a microbiology textbook from his medical school experience. While using the book to explain something about staph infections, Michael paused and said, "Wait, I need to look this up because I think this has changed," and grabbed his iPad to do so. Erik was shocked that this serious-looking nonfiction text may have something inaccurate in it and even more so that a piece of knowledge may have changed! Events such as this provide wonderful opportunities for critical conversations about the validity of what is written in nonfiction texts and the nature of knowledge.

Such conversations, whether curriculum driven or child-centered, may include questions like: Who creates knowledge? How do understandings and scientific knowledge evolve over time? How do authors come up with the information they put in books? Is it possible for books to include inaccurate or outdated information? Are all informational texts equally reliable? Even very young children can engage with such questions in productive ways and can work with their teachers and their peers toward building and sustaining a critical literacy culture in their classrooms.

CURRENT CLASSROOM PRACTICE

Such critical explorations do not seem to be a component of the reading curricula currently used in elementary schools. Though modern anthologies and guided reading book collections that are aligned with the Common Core Standards include many more nonfiction texts than their counterparts of a decade ago, the focus of instruction is for students to be able to identify and restate *what the book says*, thus showing their ability to "master complex text."

Part of the problem stems from the fact that, though some of the texts included in such programs are of decent literary quality, they are fairly traditional in their content, organization, and formatting, constructing the erroneous impression to their readers that this is the only way for informational texts to be written.

Particularly problematic in such texts is the fact that the visual content of the book (i.e., illustrations/images, font, layout) is treated like an afterthought, only marginally contributing to the informational content of what ideally should be a multimodal composition that combines both written language and image in the construction of meaning. In these books, information is primarily provided through the written text, whereas images have a merely ancillary role, only helping to clarify complex ideas from the written text or to act like a photo album of whatever topic the book is about.

So, for example, while the written text of an informational picture book about the African elephant will include a host of information about the daily lives of elephants and their habitat, its images will simply be a collection of photos of elephants that are loosely connected to what the text is talking about. As such, their role is mostly decorative, simply providing a broad visual of what the written text is talking about (see for example [Houghton Mifflin Harcourt's [2012] *A Sound in the Ground*).]

That is not at all the case with *Giant Squid* (Candace Fleming, ill. Eric Rohmann, 2016), where the written language and image content of the book are working closely together to build meaning and provide information about these peculiar creatures. So while Fleming's text succinctly states "Watch out for that barracuda! Quick! INK!" Rohmann offers a series of illustrations showing first the fearsome head of a barracuda with its heavily toothed mouth and then ink clouds that allow the squids to fool predators and dart away to safety.

Similarly, written text and image collaborate to drive home the point that there is much not yet known about these mysterious sea creatures: while Fleming's text warns readers that they "must rely on clues, as scientists do," adding that giant squids are "rarely seen . . . instead, they are merely glimpsed," Rohmann's illustrations begin with frames of menacing tentacles in dark waters and ferocious beaks, very effectively building a sense of mystery and awe. Indeed, the reader does not get a full body shot of a giant squid until several pages into the book, as a parallel affirmation of Fleming's counsel of having to rely on clues to construct our knowledge of these creatures.

It can be argued that some lapses in literary quality can be potentially forgiven of texts that are produced based on leveling algorithms and formulaic composition guidelines. After all, these texts are created as tools for teaching basic decoding and comprehension skills and do not make any claims of literary greatness. However, when such texts become the main content of students' reading diets, several problems are likely to arise.

When these are the only kinds of nonfiction text that find their way into our classrooms, it's likely that not only the students, but also the teachers get a false sense of what the genre is supposed to be like in terms of content, organization, and format, and they also learn to ignore images as irrelevant to the meaning content of the book.

Even though there may be very compelling instructional and practical reasons for including these kinds of texts in our instruction, there are urgent reasons for also including exceptional informational texts, which have the capacity to provide a broader understanding of the genre and its possibilities and can help hone students' literary judgment. Indeed, critical conversations contrasting basalized nonfiction and high-quality nonfiction in terms of aesthetic value, informativeness, and engagement can be very valuable. So too can creating experiences reading exemplary nonfiction texts as a regular part of the curriculum.

ALTERNATIVE TO CURRENT PRACTICE

Why do we read? This might seem like a trivial question halfway through a chapter focusing on critical conversations with nonfiction texts, but it is not. The authors of this chapter, Xenia and Nancy, have deeply held beliefs about the role reading plays in their lives and the lives of children. Current classroom practices in elementary classrooms across the United States that have refocused reading instruction to be about the act of reading itself, and not about the cognitive growth that results because of the content of what is read, have refocused teaching to be more about *learning to read* instead of *reading to learn.*

However, children, just like adults, are more apt to engage in reading that leads them to learn about their environments, their feelings, and their relationships with other people.

Practices that focus instruction on learning to read are steering our youth into a world where many *can* read, but *choose not to* (Altwerger, Jordan, & Shelton, 2007). Classroom practices that are structured for students to "identify the main idea and three supporting details" are quite different from lessons that require students to "identify what the text means to you, providing examples so your reader can follow your thinking."

In the former, the activity presumes that there is a single, correct message the author intends the reader to identify. The latter approach recognizes that the transaction between the reader, the reader's experience and prior knowledge, and the text may result in multiple main ideas, all connected directly to the text, but giving authority to the reader.

Externally directed literacy practices are not authentic learning experience (Shelton & Altwerger, 2015). Students engaged in authentic discussion are not limited to responding to teacher questions, always trying to guess the "correct answer" already in the teacher's mind. Instead, students are empowered to raise and pursue topics they find compelling, to invite and consider multiple points of view and interpretations, and to make connections across different experiences and different texts (Hadjioannou & Townsend, 2015).

To make this possible, teachers participate in discussions not as arbiters of correctness but as scaffolders, who model deep engagement with literary text, tolerance of tentativeness, and genuine interest in others' ideas in building richer and more nuanced understandings (Hadjioannou, 2007; Hadjioannou & Townsend, 2015).

These discussions help teachers develop a transformative stance in their teaching, which is what students need to become literate members in today's world (Shelton & Altwerger, 2015). In order to move toward a transformative stance, teachers not only need to know their students, they also need to know how to engage students in a variety of texts, including nonfiction picture books.

There is no doubt that the demands on teachers' time and energy are contributing factors in their development as self-directed and transformative teachers (Shelton & Altwerger, 2015). The following discussion is designed to provide information that can support teachers and protect their time as they infuse authentic nonfiction text reading in their curriculum in an effort to respond to their students' interests as well as their own.

As suggested earlier, the literary quality of the books we bring into our classrooms matters a great deal in stimulating student interest and engagement, in providing an accurate and comprehensive view of the genre, and in supporting the development of literary insight and aesthetic. Though all teachers should develop and have confidence in their capacity to evaluate and select good books for their students, with the multitude of available options, it is often difficult to find a good place to start looking.

Book lists of recognized, prestigious awards can be invaluable book-selection resources, since much of the text evaluation has been done for the teacher. The two most prominent nonfiction book awards are the Orbis Pictus Award (National Council of Teachers of English—NCTE) and the Sibert Award (American Library Association—ALA). Both award committees consider books published in the United States during the previous year.

Orbis Pictus books are selected by an NCTE committee with the goal of "promoting and recognizing excellence in the writing of nonfiction for children" (NCTE, 2017). As noted earlier in this chapter, nonfiction texts are "written, designed, and organized to interpret documentable, factual material for children" that naturally attracts even the youngest children. Criteria for this award include accuracy; logical, patterned organization; attractive design with illustrations that complement text; style; interesting writing; and rich language.

The Sibert Award, sponsored by the American Library Association, is designed to recognize texts that are "written and illustrated to present, organize, and interpret documentable, factual material" (ALA, 2017). Criteria for the Sibert Award include excellent use of language, excellent visual presentation, appropriate organization and information, accurate and stimulating presentation of information, appropriate style for topic and audience, supportive features, respectful and of interest to children. Given the extensive reviewing of current publications that both NCTE and the ALA conduct, it is wise to capitalize on this work to help identify books appropriate for teaching.

In order to provide an overview for current teachers, we reviewed the winning book and the honor picture books for both awards from 2012 through 2017. We then separated the books into those appropriate for early elementary grades and those for the middle grades. We'd like to emphasize that we used no quantitative criteria to determine the grade-band category in which we placed these award-winning books.

Instead, we assessed the length, complexity, and maturity of both the text and the illustrations. Furthermore, we know that a reader's "knowledge, interest, and strategic processing" (Alexander, n.d., p. 2) play active roles when comprehending texts. Therefore, we urge readers to use our recommendations only as guidelines when making decisions about the appropriateness of any text.

Early Elementary

We identified several titles that fell into three major categories of texts appropriate for young students. These biographies typically introduce little-known historic figures who have led lives that are likely to intrigue young students. In addition to the dancer, mathematician, and social activist mentioned earlier, students can also read about a poet (Pablo Neruda), a painter (Horace Pippin), an astrophysicist (Carl Sagan), and a boy who loved words (Peter Mark Roget). Although the people written about in these books led complex lives and contributed in very mature ways, the texts and illustrations are appropriate for young readers.

The three texts addressing science and nature include the aforementioned *Giant Squid* (Fleming, 2016), the fascinating encyclopedia-type *Animals by the Numbers: A Book of Animal Infographics* (Jenkins, 2016), and the absorbing bilingual concept book *¡Olinguito, de la A a la Z! Unveiling the Cloud Forest* (Delacre, 2016), which brings the reader on a journey through the enchanted forest high in the Andes mountains in the country of Ecuador.

The remaining three honored books published within this time frame and that are appropriate for young readers fall into what we categorize as books about "amusements." The first two could also join the biographies since they recount Gale Ferris's magnificent invention of the Ferris wheel (Davis, 2014) and Tony Sarg's fascination with puppetry that ended in the creation of the helium-filled balloons that continue to dominate the Macy's Thanksgiving Day Parade (Sweet, 2011). Anyone who knows children knows many are captivated by their interest in trains. *Locomotive* (Floca, 2013) chronicles a voyage across the United States in a steam locomotive in the 1800s.

Intermediate Grades

Sadly, many intermediate (and middle grade) teachers abandon the practice of reading picture books aloud to their students, erroneously assuming picture books are only for the youngest of children. During Nancy's career teaching in public schools, read-alouds were an integral component of her curriculum, regardless of the grade level she taught, including sixth grade middle school students (Shelton, 2001; Shelton & Fu, 2004).

In addition, we have found that the image content of picture books can do wonders in scaffolding the comprehension and engagement of English learners as well as students who read below grade level (Fu & Shelton, 2007; North & Shelton, 2014). And now as university professors, both Xenia and Nancy regularly read picture books aloud to college-age students and consistently receive positive feedback from them in terms of their appreciation of literature, the community that is developed within our classrooms, and their sheer enjoyment of being read to.

The fourteen award-winning picture books we placed in the intermediate-grades group are best summarized as fitting into the same three categories as the texts for younger readers; however, we also identified topics that reoccur that will enable teachers to match the books with their curriculum goals.

Every elementary school teacher in the United States studies equal rights with their students at some point in the school year. Rather than approach this topic by turning to the same historical figures year after year (i.e., Rosa Parks, Harriet Tubman, Frederick Douglass, Dr. Martin Luther King) or the same historical events (Alabama bus boycott, Underground Railroad, March on Washington), several books in this collection offer exciting alternatives that can inspire critical conversations about highlighted and suppressed narratives in history and about historical research.

Among these are a book about Fannie Lou Hamer's contribution to the civil rights movement (Weatherford, 2015), Sylvia Mendez's family's influence in desegregating schools that preceded *Brown v. Board of Education* by seven years (Tonatiuh, 2014), and Sarah Roberts, a four-year-old girl who was evicted from the Boston schools in 1847 because she was African American, but whose family fought for her rights, which resulted in the 1855 integration of Boston's public schools (Goodman, 2016). Each of these books is easily connected to oft-discussed people and events but has the additional value of opening new avenues of discussion and illustrating the wide range of people, events, and actions that brought about change.

Several of the books in this group are on STEM topics and can be readily integrated into science class. When teachers take control of the books instead of letting the books control them, a science curriculum can explode with excitement. A key suggestion for teachers who may not have experience reading nonfiction text aloud to their students is simply this: You do not have to read a book from cover to cover.

If you preread the text and determine what is appropriate for your students, your curriculum, your own knowledge, and the time you have in your schedule to share these books with your students, use paper clips and Post-its to help guide you to and through portions of a text that meet your needs.

An example of this is to integrate Cate's (2013) award-winning book about birds, Roth and Trumbone's (2013) extensive knowledge of parrots, and Burns's chapter "Winter Birding" (2012). The books can then be made available to the students to peruse through the complete text, which will, once again, encourage them to be inquisitive readers and thinkers, traits we all hope to develop in our students.

A final recommendation is for teachers to identify complementary texts and use multiple genres and multiple media when teaching any topic. Exemplary fiction texts are available in all content areas and so are websites, videos, and apps. Approaching a topic with an open mind in terms of the knowledge sources that can be explored and leveraged in the process of learning can be a powerful strategy.

Combining fiction with nonfiction literature can generate engagement with rich stories, while at the same time ensuring accurate content knowledge. Similarly, including multimedia resources can bring in real-world authenticity to topic explorations and pique the interest of children. Ultimately, such multigenre and multimedia approaches encourage critical conversations about differences in the characteristics of the various genres studied and media accessed, including the heightened accuracy demands we have of nonfiction of any medium or form.

CONCLUSION

Bringing nonfiction into the early grades classroom has been seen by some as an unjustified assault on fiction and on childhood, while others have hailed it as a much-needed turn toward serious academic learning from the very beginning of children's school lives. Though we are troubled by the narrow, formulaic treatment nonfiction texts often receive these days, we believe that exceptional nonfiction literature belongs in bookshelves, classrooms, and libraries for people of all ages.

High-quality nonfiction books have the capacity to excite and satiate the curiosity of readers, to support knowledge acquisition and reading comprehension, to develop literary insight, and to generate vital critical conversations. They also have the capacity to be great fun. As long as we honor what students find salient and make supported space for their questions and their explorations, nonfiction literature can be a most powerful genre in the literary lives of early childhood classroom communities.

NOTE

1. One of the authors of this chapter.

REFERENCES

ALA. (2017). Robert F. Sibert Informational Book Medal! Retrieved May 31, 2017, from http://www.ala.org/alsc/awardsgrants/bookmedia/sibertmedal.

Alexander, P. A. (n.d.). The path to competence: A lifespan developmental perspective on reading. Paper commissioned by the National Reading Conference.

Altwerger, B., Jordan, N., & Shelton, N. R. (2007). *Rereading fluency: Process, practice and policy.* Portsmouth, NH: Heinemann.

Fu, D., & Shelton, N. R. (2007). Including students with special needs in a writing workshop. *Language Arts, 4,* 325–336.

Hadjioannou, X. (2007). Bringing the background to the foreground: What do classroom environments that support authentic discussions look like? *American Educational Research Journal (AERJ), 44*(2), 370–399.

Hadjioannou, X., & Townsend, J. (2015). Examining booktalks to shed light on authentic classroom discussion. *Classroom Discourse, 6*(3), 198–220.

NCTE. (2017). NCTE Orbis Pictus Award for Outstanding Nonfiction for Children. Retrieved May 31, 2017, from http://www.ncte.org/awards/orbispictus.

Newkirk, T. (1989). *More than stories: The range of children's writing.* Portsmouth, NH: Heinemann.

North, C., & Shelton, N. R. (2014). Advancing English language learning in China through multimodal content area teaching. *Journal of Curriculum and Instruction, 8*(2), 68–88.

Rosenblatt, L. M. (1995). *Literature as exploration* (5th ed.). New York, NY: Modern Language Association of America.

Shelton, N. R. (2001). *Reflective teaching in an SFA classroom. Florida Reading Quarterly, 37,* 6–10.

Shelton, N. R., & Altwerger, B. (Eds.) (2015). *Literacy policies and practices in conflict: Reclaiming classrooms in networked times.* New York, NY: Routledge.

Shelton, N. R., & Fu, D. (2004). One teacher's way to create space for teaching writing and test preparation. *Language Arts, 83,* 120–128.

CHILDREN'S BOOKS CITED

Burns, L. G. (2012). Photographs by Ellen Harasimowicz. *Citizen scientist: Be a part of scientific discovery from your own backyard.* New York, NY: Henry Holt and Company.

Cate, A. L. (2013). *Look up! Bird watching in your own backyard.* Somerville, MA: Candlewick Press.

Davis, K. G. (2014). *Mr. Ferris and his wheel.* New York, NY: Houghton Mifflin Harcourt.

Delacre, L. (2016). *¡Olinguito, de la A a la Z! Unveiling the Cloud Forest.* New York, NY: Lee & Low Books.

Fleming, C. (2016). *Giant squid.* Illustrated by Eric Rohmann. New York, NY: Roaring Brook Press.

Floca, B. (2013). *Locomotive.* New York, NY: Atheneum Books for Young Readers.

Goodman, S. E. (2016). Illustrated by E. B. Lewis. *The first step: How one girl put segregation on trial.* New York, NY: Bloomsbury.

Heiligman, D. (2013). Illustrated by LeUyen Pham. *The boy who loved math: The improbable life of Paul Erdos.* New York, NY: Roaring Book Press.

Houghton Mifflin Harcourt. (2012). *A sound in the ground.* Boston, MA: Houghton Mifflin Harcourt.

Jenkins, S. (2016). *Animals by the numbers: A book of animal infographics.* New York, NY: Houghton Mifflin Harcourt.

Markel, M. (2013). Illustrated by Melissa Sweet. *Brave girl: Clara and the shirtwaist makers' strike of 1909.* New York, NY: Balzer & Bray, an imprint of HarperCollins Publishers.

Roth, S. L., & Trumbore, C. (2013). Illustrated by Susan L. Roth. *Parrots over Puerto Rico.* New York, NY: Lee & Low.

Snyder, L. (2015). Illustrated by Julie Morstad. *Swan: The life and dance of Anna Pavlova.* San Francisco, CA: Chronicle Books LLC.

Sweet, M. (2011). *Balloons over Broadway: The true story of the puppeteer of Macy's parade.* New York, NY: Houghton Mifflin Harcourt.

Tonatiuh, D. (2014). *Separate is never equal: Sylvia Mendez and her family's fight for desegregation.* New York, NY: Abrams Books for Young Readers.

Weatherford, C. B. (2015). Illustrated by Ekua Holmes. *Voice of freedom: Fannie Lou Hamer: Spirit of the civil rights movement.* Somerville, MA: Candlewick Press.

Chapter Five

Critical Questions about Photographic "Truths" in Children's Nonfiction Books

Laura Anne Hudock

In children's literature courses for prekindergarten to fourth grade teacher candidates, scenarios that intersect theory and practice are often generated from shared personal experiences of veteran elementary educators. In spring 2017, twenty-two students in such a course pondered the scenario given below along with Pinterest search results of the phrase "nonfiction chart" to inquire, "How would you respond?"

> While helming a weekly language arts meeting with the other six first grade teachers, two reading specialists, two English as second language teachers, and an instructional coach, you task these colleagues to brainstorm resources, including picture-book titles, which support unpacked grade-level curricular standards about nonfiction literature for whole class lessons. Within minutes someone suggests that you create an anchor chart like the ones on Pinterest to indicate the differences between fiction and nonfiction.

Initial comments criticized the overwhelming presentation of fiction and nonfiction as mutually exclusive—pushing back against the relationship of illustrations with fiction and photographs with nonfiction. Citing numerous counterexamples, such as Ransom Riggs's (2011) *Miss Peregrine and the Peculiar Children*, Mo Willems's *Knuffle Bunny* (2004), and Brian Floca's (2009) *Moonshot: The Flight of Apollo 11*, they fretted such teacher-made charts may mislead child readers into binary thinking and impede their future reading discoveries.

Their conversation lacked any substantial mention of the reductive descriptors of "make-believe" versus "real" or "true fact" featured on these charts. By omission these teacher candidates had acceded to the authority of photographic nonfiction books as imparter of a single, objective "truth" to be comprehended. Such privileging decontextualizes these multimodal texts' social construction and disregards readers' negotiation of "meaning potentials" (Serafini, 2014) or, as this chapter distinguishes them, "truths."

Photographs are ubiquitous. Not only do they pervade daily lives, but their trustworthiness often goes unquestioned. Cameras at intersections or tollbooths capture still images of the license plate and driver of a vehicle failing to obey traffic laws. Headshots on passports are internationally recognized as legal identification. Police release still images from closed-circuit cameras for the public to identify suspects potentially involved in criminal activity. This emphasis on photographs as conveyors of "truth" potentially muddies the waters, so to speak, of their constructed "reality" intended to visually represent particular social meanings.

Photographs are often believed to be mimetic, a mirroring of nature (Hall, 1997). Because they resemble the objects or people they represent, more so than words, they serve as powerful visual evidence to many. But an image of a vehicle should not be confused with the actual one—it is impossible to drive a photograph! Belgian surrealist René Magritte's famous painting *The Treachery of Images*, which features a visual image of a smoking pipe and caption in French, "Ceci n'est pas une pipe" (This is not a pipe), reminds viewers of this irreconcilable contradiction. Magritte's visual representation is *not* an actual pipe to smoke, just an artistic likeness of one.

Borrowing from semiotics, a photograph—an icon—is a particular kind of mimetic signifier that is perceived as closely resembling the person, place, or object to which it refers. Every instance a reader transacts with a photograph in a particular social context, meaning is realized by way of his or her relationship to that for which it stands (Chandler, 2002; Serafini, 2014). For example, the iconicity of Dorothea Lange's famous Depression-era photograph, *Migrant Mother*, has become quite conventionalized within American culture as representing poverty and hunger; it should not be mistaken for a singular "truth."

The presentation of this iconic photograph for a particular context, such as a child reading one of several available biographies about Lange in a school setting, mediates multiple possible interpretational "truths." The conclusion of Weatherford's (2017) biography situates the making of Lange's iconic photograph as a catalyst for national attention and governmental intervention. In another biography that highlights Lange's steadfast efforts to make visible the faces of those enduring this poverty and hunger, Rosenstock (2016) writes in the sole red font, "The truth, seen with love, becomes Dorothea's art" (n.p.).

Given the ongoing barrage of digital images in daily lives, out of necessity, instructional practices at any grade level should embrace the space needed to purposefully explore photographs in children's nonfiction books. To prepare teacher candidates for current and future critical visual literacy demands, the open-ended design of this inquiry experience works toward disrupting the hegemony of photographs as a singular "truth."

THE INQUIRY EXPERIENCE

Going beyond mere teacher-directed "show-and-tell" activities (Duffelmeyer & Ellertson, 2006), this inquiry situates students as adept composers and informed readers of nonfiction picture books. From snapping photographs and brainstorming topics to writing verbal text and composing page layouts, teacher candidates partook in every step of book production. Then they responded to each other's finalized nonfiction books and applied their knowledge to evaluating other published titles. An open-ended survey documented their personal reflections on this learning experience.

Along the way students' agentic voices emerged. This inquiry positioned them to subsequently interrogate, or read against, photographic nonfiction literature for children that would have likely been accepted as prima facie "real" or "true fact." With written permission, this chapter details these teacher candidates' inquiry experience and postinquiry discoveries that pose critical questions about photographic "truths" in children's nonfiction books.

Ways of Seeing Photographs

To begin this experiential learning opportunity, it is incumbent upon the instructor to informally gauge the learners' particular ways of seeing, their "interpretation and critical inquiry into the meaning potential of visual images" (Serafini, 2014, p. 167). Projecting a digital image of David Carson's Pulitzer Prize–winning photograph and purposefully withholding the circumstances at the site of production and critical reception, teacher candidates metacognitively reflected on what they see, wonder, feel, think, and notice (McGregor, 2007). Sharing aloud their interpretations, they rationalized their ways of seeing by invoking feelings, relating to prior life experiences, or citing visual clues.

As if they had been transported to vicariously experience a singular moment in time, some remarked on how they felt energized from the photographed crowd. Another speculated if the photograph's subjects were, indeed, spectators standing with their arms raised as part of a rhythmic wave. Given the reflective lighting and implied nighttime, one teacher candidate even wondered if the photograph was taken at a concert venue. Noticing the street signs, several refuted that particular interpretation, instead deeming it a block party.

Identified visual clues merely affirmed that which is familiar to these students' everyday lives and discourses. Each teacher candidate's sociocultural positioning shaped each interpretation. Photographs are, ultimately, ideological texts imbued with meaning within the recognized boundaries of a particular sociocultural group or community. Every photograph, whether featured on social media, news media, or in nonfiction books, is grounded in a particular view of the world (Gee, 2011).

Table 5.1.   Critical Visual Literacy Survey

Question 1
Reflect on the **process** of making your nonfiction book. First, describe your process. Next, consider the following: Who is your intended audience? How did your group decide? How did your group choose photographs to feature? Text to write? What design features did your group consider? Why? What posed the greatest challenge? And what are you most proud of?

Question 2
What are your personal discoveries about the experience of creating a nonfiction book with photographs? How might your learning and/or discoveries impact your future teaching with or about nonfiction literature for children?

Question 3
What did you notice about the final products—the various nonfiction books?

Question 4
Given the opportunity, what might you do differently when creating a nonfiction book?

Question 5
What did you discover about how readers respond to photographic nonfiction books? How might your discoveries impact your future teaching with or about nonfiction literature for children?

Question 6
Please provide any additional a-HAs, comments, insights, highlights, feedback, or reactions to this critical visual literacy experience.

Revealing the photograph's contextualizing caption, distinction, and an impromptu gathering of information, that is, a newspaper article titled "Attacked on the Job: A Post-Dispatch Photographer's Tale" (Hunn, 2014), and a local television interview, vocalizations of shock, anger, and embarrassment materialized among these teacher candidates.

Such disclosures weren't intended to disparage students' initial ways of seeing, their failure to recognize the inception of the Black Lives Matter movement on the streets of Ferguson, Missouri, but rather to uncover the range of interpretive "truths" negotiated from a single photograph. "I can't believe I thought that," commented Alyssa[1] about her subjective interpretation. "I mean, that [discourse] didn't even cross my mind."

Afterward teacher candidates closely read and discussed photographs in dozens of nonfiction books that they individually borrowed from children's libraries. Each selected one or two photographs to consider various possible interpretations occurring within small groups. Informing the next steps of this inquiry, their conversational musings primarily focused on book production and reception. In short, they collectively wondered how photographs in children's nonfiction books are composed and selected to communicate certain viewpoints, "truths," through visual representations of people, places, things, and events to a particular implied audience of readers.

Nonfiction Book Production

Unanimously agreeing to create their own nonfiction books for children, these teacher candidates further chose to take their own photographs too. Their enthusiasm soon faded into a barrage of logistical questions. The infinite photographic possibilities daunted them. To retain ample creative choice, the class limited their photography to the week of spring break. Subject matter would include places, things, and events. However, due to obtaining permissions, photographs of people were limited to just classmates.

Instead of uploading these photographs to a course-specific online learning platform, students desired to see each other's photographs straightaway. In addition, they wanted to use the editing tools and filters familiar to them. And so they opted to create a private Instagram account that only students enrolled in the course and their instructor could access. Their nonfiction books would feature selections from the two dozen photographs uploaded to Instagram.

Photographic Selection

For the next three classes collaborative planning, research, and book design occurred. Nearly every student immediately scoured Instagram to seek inspiration. Deciding on a topic seemed to be the first hurdle. Seeking a unified theme from among the photographs, their suggested topics included teacher's pets, happiness, and spring break. Of the latter, some groups opted to focus on destinations, activities, or a general overview of the collegiate spring break experience. Upon reflection Haddie remarked, "The hardest part of the book was deciding which pictures to portray and what message we wanted to get across for the book as a whole."

Most groups cherry-picked from among the photographs that supported their chosen topic. But to ensure that no photographer felt excluded, two of the six groups incorporated all of the photographs. "We found a way to group all of the pictures together," explains Nathalie. She writes in her online survey, "we selected all of them, [sic] because all of the pictures showed our classmates doing things that make them happy." Such inclusiveness proved challenging to Nathalie's group in their organizational use of "sub-themes (pets, traveling, service, etc.)." The second group constructed a collage on their book's last page.

Assumptions about Implied Child Readers

Some teacher candidates gathered information about certain photographs. They'd ask a classmate, "Hey, where did you take that picture?" or "What's the name of your dog?" Others conducted web searches to locate destinations. Not until typing out the words for their nonfiction books did these groups settle on an intended audience of child readers. Such considerations were absent from their initial selections of photographs to feature.

Since these photographs were taken for a children's literature class, any censoring of subject matter likely occurred prior to posting on Instagram; thus, they trustingly deemed all photographs to be appropriate and fair game for inclusion in their nonfiction books. After all, not a single raucous spring break party appeared among them.

Nathalie's group decided to showcase "some background knowledge on spring break because we realize that the reader may be unfamiliar." Her group assumed that either the implied child reader may lack familiarity with their topic or their nonfiction book may serve as an authoritative resource on information about spring break activities. Another assumption centered on the implied child reader's literacy skills. Avalyn's group envisioned "first graders who have never been on spring break." Her partner, Haley, wrote a detailed explanation that reflected on the influence of this assumption on their nonfiction book's layout, design, and word choice:

> My partner and I decided to make our book simple. Each page had a picture of what someone in the class did on spring break. The words were the same on each page except for a few. The line always started with "Some people on spring break . . ." and then it would say what the person in the picture was doing. . . . Each page was set up with a picture and text under it. We found a fun border and had that on the edges of each page.[2]

Responses to Peers' Nonfiction Books

Choosing from a limited number of photographs uploaded to Instagram, duplications among student-produced nonfiction books were bound to occur. By the second or third exchange of finalized versions of nonfiction books be-tween groups this realization took hold. Even so, Sharon notes, "we all used various formats and pieces of information to create our own unique books." Avalyn appreciated how "[n]o two books were alike." Varying topics, page design, and paired text yielded different "truths" about identical photographs.

Figures 5.2 and 5.3, two-page spreads excerpted from separate nonfiction books, exemplify this occurrence. Each book's compositional layout positions readers to interpret a single photograph in different ways. In one photograph, an apple blocks the holder's face, shrouding recognition of identity and emotional

Some people on
spring break
participate in
community
service.

Figure 5.1. Excerpted page from a student-made nonfiction book for children. *Source*: Students in Laura Hudock's Spring 2017 children's literature class.

Figure 5.2. Excerpted two-page spread from a student-made nonfiction book for children. *Source:* Students in Laura Hudock's Spring 2017 children's literature class.

Traveling Home (Abroad).

Some students are international students and for this break they get a chance to travel home and see their families and friends!

Figure 5.3. Excerpted two-page spread from a student-made nonfiction book for children. *Source*: Students in Laura Hudock's Spring 2017 children's literature class.

expression. Absence of eye contact likely positions the reader as an observer in search of other available verbal or visual clues to facilitate meaning making.

An integrated page layout in figure 5.2 overlaps words atop an unbound visual image, that is, a childlike crayon illustration that bleeds to the pages' edges and fuses them together as one unit (Painter, Martin, & Unsworth, 2013, p. 100). Superimposed within this inviting unit are scattered photographs, including the one described on p. 54, contained within rectangular frames cropped to various shapes and sizes. Each photograph's random placement potentially minimizes its interpretive weight. Readers may skip from photograph to photograph, rely more heavily on the verbal text, and, as a result, perhaps, surmise a "fat" smile exists behind that apple as a depiction of happiness.

Figure 5.3 has a complementary two-page layout (Painter, Martin, & Unsworth, 2013). The photograph on the verso, left page, faces the unbounded text block on the recto, right page. Centrally focused on their respective pages, this composition places equal weight on the visual and verbal elements within the space. The text's mention of international students going home over spring break potentially indicates the photograph's circumstantial context and apple holder's general identity.

POSTINQUIRY DISCOVERIES

In the weeks that followed this inquiry students' explorations of children's nonfiction books for various in-class activities and written assignments indicated a heightened attentiveness to photographs. Exhibiting a newfound confidence that arose from their experiential learning, teacher candidates proceeded to voice critical questions about photographic "truths" that would have otherwise gone unnoticed. Table 5.2 lists the overarching critical questions related to each categorical discovery—evaluating photo credits, assumptions about implied child readers, and reading against a photographic nonfiction book. Repeatedly prompting, "How do you know?" or "Why do you think that?" students were encouraged to articulate their deliberations.

Evaluating Photo Credits

While reviewing nonfiction trade books intended for emergent or early readers, teacher candidates encountered *Sisters* by Lola M. Schaefer (1999) from their instructor's first grade classroom library. Photo credits, listed in small print at the very end of this book, attribute numerous photographers and company sources.

Drawing on their experience of selecting photographs, an impromptu small group discussion raised several questions about this book's purpose, accuracy, and authenticity.

- Why did the author, or publisher, opt for photographs from different photographers or companies and what were their criteria for inclusion?
- How can a reader be sure the photographed subjects feature siblings, not friends?
- Why does the book only depict smiling, physically able-bodied children?

Inclusion of photo credits continued to perplex another small group of teacher candidates when evaluating Keating's (2016) *Pink Is for Blobfish*. They speculated that photographic selection may have been based on a requirement of each living thing's shared color attribute. Their scribbled phrases on a Post-it note stuck to a two-page spread about pinktoe tarantulas suggest that the

Table 5.2.   Critical Questions about Photographic "Truths"

Evaluating Photo Credits

- For what purpose(s) and in what context(s) have these photographs been taken?
- Why have these photographs been selected for inclusion in this nonfiction book?

Assumptions about Implied Child Readers

- What assumptions about implied child readers might have informed photographic content?

Reading against Nonfiction Books

- What sociocultural views does this photographic nonfiction book for children privilege, marginalize, or ignore?

amoeba-like "window frames each photograph" and "reinforces the reader's distant observation." Uncertainty about each photograph's context, taken in nature or captivity, pervaded their conversation.

Even for a photographer familiar to students, Brandon Stanton of *Humans of New York* blog fame, queries about his nonfiction book for children, *Little Humans* (2014), arose. Under what circumstances and location did he photograph these children? How did he select children to photograph and which photographs to publish? Despite careful scrutiny of Stanton's nonfiction book, including its peritext—endpapers, title page, copyright information, and removable cover—students determined that the book lacked any available information to address their queries. Only a web search yielded interviews that provided further insights into his process.

Proper attribution of sources is, of course, a necessary practice, but teacher candidates debated photo credits' potential benefit to young children's meaning making. In searching for a better way to communicate background and source information, they favored Houghton Mifflin Harcourt's Scientists in the Field series, specifically, Robert F. Sibert Informational Book Medal winner and Orbis Pictus Award for Outstanding Nonfiction for Children recommended book, *Kakapo Rescue: Saving the World's Strangest Parrot*.

In this nonfiction book author Sy Montgomery and photographer Nic Bishop (2010) embark on a ten-day excursion to remote Codfish Island to join the National Kakapo Recovery Team in their attempt to save the dwindling avian population.

Montgomery's narrative field notes blend science and natural history. She details her firsthand encounters with this flightless, nocturnal parrot and the conservation efforts to protect them. Bishop's photographs capture not only the flora and fauna of this southern New Zealand, bush-covered island through vivid close-ups and alluring landscapes, but also action shots of the scientists at work. To these teacher candidates, Bishop's photographic process embodies transparency.

Likewise, in his nonfiction early reader *Frogs*, Bishop (2015) candidly explains his amphibious encounters to child readers in a backmatter section, "A Closer Look with Nic Bishop." He writes:

To take the photographs for this book, I raised some frogs at home, caring for them as they grew from tadpoles. A few, like gliding frogs, are now favorite pets. They wake me at night with gentle singing. I found other frogs by exploring the ponds and swamps near my home. I also visited rain forests, where I was amazed by the many colors of dart poison frogs, as tiny as jelly beans on the ground! My favorite, though, was the glass frog. It was as small as a pea, with thin legs and delicate toes. You can see it on page three of this book. (p. 28)

Unlike the detached array of photographs appearing in *Sisters* (Schaefer, 1999), Bishop lends credibility of origin and conveys intentionality behind his selections. Readers become cognizant of his experiences' and preferences' influence on his featured photographs.

Assumptions about Implied Child Readers

A few weeks after the inquiry experience concluded, one teacher candidate, Alyssa, critically read *Branded by the Pink Triangle*, Setterington's (2013) Stonewall Honor Book that chronicles the experiences and persecution of gay men and lesbians in Nazi Germany. Although the nonfiction book includes historic images, advertisements, cartoons, and magazine covers, Alyssa communicated her unease regarding an apparent obscurity, an informational gap between photograph and printed text.

A black-and-white photograph of a concentration camp's stark medical lab appears opposite Holocaust survivor Richard Grune's (1947) etching titled "Solidarity" of one prisoner collapsing into the arms of another and another photograph of three poles at Sachsenhausen concentration camp from which prisoners were torturously hung by their wrists (Setterington, 2013, pp. 62–63). Alyssa's reluctance to resign these photographs to a cursory glance bespoke the considerable influence of the earlier inquiry experience.

Perceiving an absence of graphic visual content, she contemplated whether the implied child reader might be emblematic of authorial censorship of the Holocaust's atrocities. Captions reiterate the horrors mentioned in the text that these prisoners experienced in the depicted settings. In lieu of direct photographic evidence of maltreatment, only inferencing may connect verbal text to visual representation.

Her shared analysis itemized visual elements that likely assist child readers to make such inferences. An ambiance of low saturation imparts a feeling of restraint, not excitement, consistent with subject matter. Black-and-white coloring also distances the reader from the past. Alyssa recognized how young readers had been positioned to safely "create their own mental images of what happened" in those unspeakable contexts.

Reading against a Photographic Nonfiction Book

Soon after publication teacher candidates acquired a copy of Parker's (2017) *Strong Is the New Pretty: A Celebration of Girls Being Themselves* to peruse. This photographic essay presents an assemblage of portraits, action photographs, and quotes from two hundred representative North American girls to encourage implied girl readers to just be their strong selves. Marketed across various media outlets as a "natural" portrayal of girls, as the back cover says, "being 100 percent themselves," to some professional reviewers Parker's photographic project and related book embodies empowerment (Lowin, 2017; Stephenson, 2014).

Inspired by capturing her own daughters from behind the camera lens to show them "as they were, and how they were amazing" (p. 2), Parker, a professional photographer, has conceptualized this nonfiction book to become her means to disrupt the perpetuation of socially constructed gender stereotypes. She specifies her intention for this book:

> I wanted to show my girls that beauty isn't about being a certain size, or having your hair done (or even brushed, in their case), or wearing a fancy outfit. I wanted to combat the messages the media sends to women every day. I wanted my girls to know that being themselves is beautiful, and that being beautiful is about being strong. (p. 2)

Equating strong with other ways of being—confident, wild, resilient, creative, determined, kind, fearless, joyful, and independent—Parker arranges her selected photographs by these categorical relations.

To these teacher candidates, critical readers, a quote from nine-year-old Ella, the swimmer featured on the front cover and later in the book, shatters the guise of this premise to reveal a photograph's perceived contrivance of confidence-building. Ella, presumably one of Parker's daughters, states:

> I was really scared for my first triathlon. My mom took this shot of me the night before and told me that even though I was afraid to race, to try to *look* tough and fearless. I did, and when my mom showed me this shot, it made me believe I could be as tough as I look. (p. 17)

The heavy-handed staging of this photograph as well as the construction of a photographic "truth" that privileges a certain perspective on girlhood may be gleaned from this excerpt. Parker's instructions about the resulting body language and facial expression of dogged determination contradict her daughter's conveyance of nervousness, thus leading students to wonder why Parker denied photographic acknowledgment of her daughter's anxiety the night before her first race. And why would such an emotional state be deemed undesirable for girls?

Blatantly ignoring the idiom "don't judge a book by its cover," teacher candidates also attended to the visual composition of the book's title. White lettering of "Strong" and "Pretty" against a solid black background assigns equal importance to these words. As Ella's steely eyes demand a reader's gaze, she exudes strength while positioning readers to enter her world, albeit a potentially fictitious one. Her coveted thin, sculpted arms and tanned skin radiate culturally defined markers of mainstream American beauty for Caucasian women of all ages.

While questioning the duality of these photographic "truths" on the front cover, concretized by the title's font color, students bemoaned the possibility of "strong" becoming a semantic substitute for "pretty" and therefore fixing yet another societal standard for girls to project. Even so, the exquisite portraitures' aesthetic appeal won their hearts but failed to sway their minds. These critically visual literate teacher candidates recognized Parker's photographs as deliberate sociocultural constructions of and not transparent windows on "reality."

Akin to Toto pulling back the curtain to reveal an ordinary man fabricating the lore of the great and powerful Wizard of Oz in the cinematic motion picture, critical visual literacy requires students to lift the "ideological veil" by way of their own interrogations about photographic nonfiction literature for children (Mitchell, 2002, p. 170). As a result of this inquiry experience, evidenced by their postinquiry discoveries, teacher candidates no longer accepted photographs at face value. They generated their own questions to guide their negotiations of photographic "truths" while making and reading children's nonfiction books.

Inquiry awakened students' sense of wonder. It opened spaces for them to challenge the authority of photographs as an undisputed conveyor of "truth." And most significantly, it enabled them to "develop and exercise the critically literate characteristic of feeling agency" when confronting conventionalized meanings (Duffelmeyer & Ellertson, 2006, n.p.). Building students' capacities to systematically interrogate the production, reception, and power of photographs in children's nonfiction books has been the key to unlocking these "truths."

NOTES

1. All names of teacher candidates participating in this inquiry experience are pseudonyms.

2. Figure 5.1 shows an excerpted page from their nonfiction book.

REFERENCES

Chandler, D. (2002). *Semiotics: The basics.* New York, NY: Routledge.

Duffelmeyer, B. B., & Ellertson, A. (2006). Critical visual literacy: Multimodal communication across the curriculum. *Across the Disciplines: A Journal of Language, Learning, and Academic Writing, 3*. Retrieved from https://wac.colostate.edu/atd/.

Gee, J. P. (2011). *Social linguistics and literacies: Ideology in discourses.* 4th edition. New York, NY: Routledge.

Hall, S. (Ed.). (1997). *Representation: Cultural representations and signifying practices.* London, UK: Sage.

Hunn, D. (August 11, 2014). Attacked on the job: A *Post-Dispatch* photographer's tale. *St. Louis Post-Dispatch.* Retrieved from http://www.stltoday.com.

Lowin, R. (March 8, 2017). Photographer empowers girls everywhere with "Strong Is the New Pretty." *NBCUniversal Media.* Retrieved from http://www.today.com.

McGregor, T. (2007). *Comprehension connections: Bridges to strategic reading.* Portsmouth, NH: Heinemann.

Mitchell, W. J. T. (2002). Showing seeing: A critique of visual culture. *Journal of Visual Culture, 1*(2), 165–181.

Painter, C., Martin, J. R., & Unsworth, L. (2013). *Reading visual narratives: Image analysis of children's picture books.* Oakville, CT: Equinox.

Serafini, F. (2014). *Reading the visual: An introduction to teaching multimodal literacy.* New York, NY: Teachers College Press.

Stephenson, M. A. (May 28, 2014). Strong is the new pretty: What beauty looks like in the next generation of girls [blog post]. *The Huffington Post.* Retrieved from http://www.huffingtonpost.com/.

CHILDREN'S BOOKS CITED

Bishop, N. (2015). *Frogs.* New York, New York, NY: Scholastic.

Floca, B. (2009). *Moonshot: The flight of Apollo 11.* New York, NY: Atheneum Books for Young Readers.

Keating, J. (2016) *Pink is for blobfish.* New York, NY: Alfred A. Knopf.

Montgomery, S. (2010). *Kakapo rescue: Saving the world's strangest parrot.* Boston, MA: Houghton Mifflin Books for Children.

Parker, K. T. (2017) *Strong is the new pretty: A celebration of girls being themselves.* New York, NY: Workman Publishing.

Riggs, R. (2011). *Miss Peregrine and the peculiar children.* Philadelphia, PA: Quirk Books.

Rosenstock, B. (2016). *Dorothea's eyes: Dorothea Lange photographs the truth.* Honesdale, PA: Calkins Creek.

Schaefer, L. M. (1999). *Sisters.* Mankato, MN: Pebble Books.

Setterington, K. (2013). *Branded by the pink triangle.* Toronto, ON: Second Story Press.

Stanton, B. (2014). *Little humans.* New York, NY: Farrar, Straus, Giroux.

Weatherford, C. B. (2017). *Dorothea Lange: The photographer who found the faces of the Depression.* Chicago, IL: Albert Whitman & Company.

Willems, M. (2004). *Knuffle bunny.* New York, NY: Hyperion Books for Children.

Chapter Six

Science Inquiry in a Fifth Grade Classroom

Shanetia P. Clark and Vincent Genareo

A lively group of fifth graders pile into the science lab. They rush to their seats, excited about coming into the science lab. Six tables, each with four blue stools, fill with eager boys and girls. Mrs. Morris shepherds the students into the room, urging, "Come in quickly. We have a full block today. Go to the shelves to get your science notebooks, your journals, and your pencils."

Upon entering the fifth grade science lab, this class sees shelves of trade books about polar bears, the weather, and ocean animals. Counters are stacked with other trade books that supplement the textbook. The back table houses examples of student work—dioramas detailing the earth's layers, artistic renderings of the different types of stars, and the beginning workings for the creation of a reader's theater about climate change. Posters line the wall, reminding the students of "What Good Scientists Do" and the types of "Big Questions." Supplies are stacked in box crates from floor to ceiling. This room is a scientific feast for the eyes.

"Boys and girls, please look to the board. Before we begin our investigation, I want you to think about the statements about beaver dams on the board. Do you agree with them? Why or why not? In your notebook, write down your thinkings about the statements. We'll discuss in our table groups and as a class in five minutes." The students hurriedly write their thoughts in their science journals.

After five minutes, Mrs. Morris announces, "Okay, everyone. Now talk with your tablemates about your thinking." A chorus of talk rises in the lab. Students share their notebooks. Mrs. Morris pops into each group to listen to their discussions. Next, she calls the class to order and whole-class discussion begins. Soon they will begin an experiment testing the hypothesis generated in the discussion.

CONTEXT

District Elementary School[1] is one of five elementary schools in the Coastal County Public School District, which is located in a small town on the upper shore of the Eastern Shore of Maryland. This school was built in the 1970s and has an open floor plan. Classrooms do not have doors and four enclosed walls; instead, the classrooms are separated by bookshelves, cabinets, and partial walls. District Elementary School enrolls students from prekindergarten through fifth grade. (See tables 6.1 to 6.3 for details about the enrollment characteristics for District Elementary School.[2]) District Elementary School has Title I status and provides breakfast for all of its students free of charge.

The 2016 Maryland School Report Card indicated that the science proficiency of fifth grade District Elementary School students was on an upward trend, according to results on the Maryland School Assessment science test (see table 6.4 for percentages). In 2016, the fifth grade students in District Elementary School performed higher than the district average for advanced and proficient science scores (83.6 percent compared to 72.9 percent, respectively).

Table 6.1.   District Elementary School Enrollment by Grade

	Pre-K	Kindergarten	Grade 1	Grade 2	Grade 3	Grade 4	Grade 5
Students	60	97	95	102	103	98	110

Source: Maryland State Department of Education (2017).

Table 6.2.   District Elementary School Enrollment Enrollment by Race

	American Indian/Alaskan	Asian	Black	Hispanic	White	HI/Pacific Islander	Two or More
Students	0	14	105	47	432	0	67

Source: Maryland State Department of Education (2017).

Table 6.3.   District Elementary School Enrollment by Gender

	Male	Female
Students	341	324

Source: Maryland State Department of Education (2017).

Table 6.4. District Elementary School Maryland State Assessment: Science Results

	2014	*2015*	*2016*
Proficient (%)	59.3	60.8	67.3
Advanced (%)	8.1	12.4	16.4
Advanced + proficient (%)	67.4	73.2	83.6

Source: Maryland State Department of Education (2017).

The 2016 science proficiency levels represented the highest percentage of advanced and proficient fifth grade District Elementary School students since 2008, when the test was first given.

This chapter focuses on the science lab program that began in the 2016–2017 academic school year. District Elementary School was selected to pilot a program in which students in grades three through five leave their regular classrooms for a science lab. Science has been taken out of the regular classroom. They have forty-five minutes of science each day with the science teacher in the science lab. This shift to place increased attention on science is due both to the 2013 Maryland implementation of the Next Generation Science Standards (NGSS) and the school and district administrations' commitment to science.

There are three teachers at District Elementary School who teach science— Christine Jones, Patty Morris, and Jen Jenkins.[3] Two were previously fourth grade teachers and one was the technology teacher. We interviewed two of the teachers, Christine and Patty. The third was unavailable due to being away on maternity leave.

Christine Jones, who was known as District Elementary School's technology teacher for the past six years, is in her first year teaching third and fifth grade science. She has enjoyed this move to teaching science. When the coauthors visited her lab, she noted that "she doesn't have as much on her walls as [Patty]." Prior to her joining the District Elementary School faculty, she taught middle school reading interventions in the neighboring public school districts.

Patty Morris, who has a gentle Georgia accent, has been teaching at the elementary level for thirty years. In this capacity, she has taught science and "everything else." With a twinkle in her eye, she added, "Except this year, I'm just teaching science, which I absolutely love . . . just teaching science because kids love it."

In addition to the increased emphasis on the science standards, the science lab format filled a strategic school need. Prior to the lab, classroom teachers were losing both individual and collaborative planning time. Therefore, in order to allocate an additional forty-five minutes of personal planning time and to advance the STEM and STEAM initiatives of the district, a change needed to occur—take science out of the regular elementary classroom and into science labs.

Christine noted with a smile, "Again, this program is extraordinary, because with the push for reading/language arts and math, social studies and science have been pushed to the outside. Now the teachers are forced to have science every day." Patty continued, "When I taught fourth grade, social studies and science were either limited or eliminated based on the day. At times, math may run long, and something would have to give." Now, science time is not impeded upon, and the classroom teachers have more opportunities to plan for and teach the other three core subjects.

We discovered that these science teachers have noted a positive shift in their pedagogy and in their students' engagement, which will be discussed in the later sections. The Next Generation Science Standards support the teachers' pedagogical stances. Moreover, the teachers were empowered to adapt and supplement the district curriculum in ways that support students' learning.

The following sections outline the background of the Next Generation Science Standards, the notion of scientific truths, and the exploration of how these teachers engage students' critical thinking with nonfiction texts to explore scientific truths.

BACKGROUND

The Next Generation Science Standards were designed to move away from science instruction that covered isolated facts and instead focus on interrelated concepts, problem solving, and authentic science and engineering practices (Krajcik, Codere, Dahsah, Bayer, & Mun, 2014). The term *practices* differs from terminology in previous standards (e.g., *scientific process or inquiry*) because it is understood that scientific engagement within each practice includes both knowledge and skills.

The Next Generation Science Standards science and engineering practices #1 (Asking questions [for science] and defining problems [for engineering]) and #8 (Obtaining, evaluating, and communicating information) explicitly require students to read from and draw on scientific texts to evaluate and communicate information (NGSS Release, 2013, p. 1). Teaching the practices of science, as demanded by the Next Generation Science Standards, means students must think and work like scientists.

To do so, "it is essential to recognize that this entails much more than learning facts and established theories. . . . It means developing habits and attitudes for inquiry [and] refining reasoning practices and abilities" (Hammer, 1995, p. 394). Patty and Christine deliberately created a learning space wherein scientific language, practices, and thinking were the norm.

Through the Next Generation Science Standards, students are taught to be critical consumers of information and read grade-appropriate, nonfiction texts with scientific information, critically analyze what they read, and use the information to answer their questions. These directives raise a number of curricular and pedagogical questions. How do students view scientific truth? How are scientific truths expressed in texts? What nonfiction texts are available for science elementary teachers?

SCIENTIFIC TRUTH

The idea of *truth* in science is problematic both in definition and epistemology. More important than what truth means in the realm of scientific knowledge is how students view scientific truth and their place within its construction. Students approach science learning with *scientific epistemological views* (SEV) (Hammer, 1995). Tsai (1999) believed "it is likely that students' [scientific epistemological views] will shape their metalearning assumptions when learning science" (p. 655).

This claim means that children's scientific epistemological views influence their understanding about their place within the knowledge construction process, their ability to challenge scientific assumptions, and learning strategies they apply to learn the content.

Children may situate scientific truth in the scientific epistemological view of *logical positivism*, one that accepts universal scientific truth and facts as concrete, stagnant, and unquestionable. In turn, these children may believe that scientific truth equates to a set of facts that can be memorized, but not questioned.

Alternatively, children may approach scientific truth from the scientific epistemological view of *scientific constructivism*, where they accept malleability of facts and interpretation. Active engagement in the scientific process will develop these students' scientific learning; they can scrutinize current views of scientific truth, test hypotheses, develop group consensus, and maintain control of their own learning.

These students understand that scientific truth changes, as it has throughout history, through the process of inquiry and discovery. It is believed by many, such as Klosterman (2016), that we should approach all truth with uncertainty. It may be argued that everything once believed to be true in science has been, or will be, demonstrated incorrect or inaccurate.

SCIENTIFIC TRUTH AND TEXTS

The National Science Teachers Association (2017) posits, "[Reading] science trade books [is] the perfect way for students to build literacy skills while learning science content." Therefore, questions of the types of text that teachers should use in the science classroom are constant. While some suggest that fiction texts should be eliminated or limited in science classrooms (Rice, 2002), others see the value of both fiction—particularly science or speculative fiction—and nonfiction in the classroom.

Science fiction imagines a world and technologies that are not yet (Kiefer & Tyson, 2013). It is valued because "scientists are born and raised to be skeptical—and that's all that much of this writing is. Being skeptical about the pure goodness of scientific advances. Sci-fi also provides a venue for discerning how our ways of thinking about science have developed historically" (Waters, 2011, paras. 3–4).

It also stimulates readers' curiosity and the capacity for invention and presents the reader with moral and ethical dilemmas that correspond to the real world. We acknowledge the need for providing high-quality science (speculative) fiction to students. As with all texts brought into the classrooms, elementary teachers should exercise thoughtful and deliberate evaluations.

If used for classroom instruction, teachers have the opportunity and obligation to illuminate scientific concepts within. For example, fictional texts that are not classified as science fiction may contain science concepts, yet they focus on developing engaging and entertaining plots, characters, and artwork. In a foundational study, Mayer (1995) researched second grade children who read the book *Dear Mr. Blueberry* (James, 1991).

In this colorfully illustrated fiction text, scientific facts were presented about Mr. Blueberry, a whale. Although the book was written to help alleviate common misconceptions about whales, it actually impeded children's learning. The scientifically inaccurate drawings and storylines (such as whales jumping across water sources) and the anthropomorphism of the whale created very little factual learning among the students, and they actually developed additional misconceptions. Generally, the students learned the story, but not the science.

Young people should also gain access to high-quality nonfiction texts. Teachers must engage critical lenses to make sure that these texts are accurate because even some elementary nonfiction science texts are not without fault. Nonfiction elementary science texts have evolved over the previous four decades to display more scientific data in the form of graphical representations of data, including flow diagrams, tree diagrams, and cutaways (Coleman & Dantzler, 2016).

When nonfiction texts are integrated in science curricula, it is noted that students can engage in higher-level thinking strategies, such as engaging in inquiry, activating prior knowledge, categorizing, analyzing, and challenging their personal assumptions (Doiron, 1994; Job & Coleman, 2016). Even so, Ford (2006) examined forty-four science trade books, a majority being nonfiction instructional texts, and found that scientific knowledge was presented as facts and little attention was given to scientific analysis, theory, or knowledge production. Even nonfiction texts may blur the line of fiction, using fictional characters or storylines to present factual information (Gill, 2009). Thus, it is fundamentally important that science teachers read, critique, and evaluate texts that they bring into the classrooms.[4]

THE STUDY

This qualitative study examined two teachers in a rural school in Maryland. It represented a unique case in that this district provided the elementary students with their own daily science laboratory period taught by science teachers. We employed a descriptive study approach and oriented our study through a social constructivist lens that accepts that people make meaning of their realities through their own unique experiences, interactions, and contexts (Creswell, 2018). Two elementary science teachers, Christine and Patty, who were mentioned earlier in the chapter, were involved in this study.

District Elementary School is a professional development school that partnered with our university, Salisbury University. The first author is a liaison to this school, which gave her the opportunity to meet the teachers, observe the science laboratories, and request interviews with the participants. Prior to the interview, the teachers toured the authors through their classrooms, where they showed examples of student projects and classroom science texts. During the recorded interview, both teachers were interviewed using formal, semistructured formats. In a peer debriefing session, the authors established themes that emerged from the responses and compared the findings with existing literature.

DEVELOPING STUDENTS' SCIENTIFIC TRUTH

Scientific truth, by the teachers' own definition, was "about the data [students] are collecting. They have to prove it. Whatever their data proves, because that's what they have to write about, as little scientists. It's what truth have they found out here." However, their classroom texts tended to present scientific truths as fact-based—the tradition of logical positivism.

These teachers used a combination of nonfiction texts in their elementary science labs. They used the STEMscopes (Accelerated Learning, 2017) curriculum, which provided short, fact-based readings meant to inform students about scientific data, connect what they read with language arts concepts (such as main idea and supporting points), and provide an introduction for subsequent discovery learning.

The teachers also enhanced their curriculum with readings they found online to support the students' learning in the lesson. Christine explained, "Sometimes we feel like we need to add in a little bit more. For a High Altitude lesson, Patty found an article. I found an article. We combined the articles to make one article. We do a lot of that." They used no trade books because they contained too much information not required for their standards. Patty noted, "Because there's so much to teach . . . we have not even come close to finishing [the year's curriculum]. A huge concern has been getting all the standards in."

However, the teachers and students found a way to use their nonfiction readings to allow for scientific discovery in the tradition of scientific constructivism. Due to the excitement that students exhibited as they learned new scientific information, the students sought additional nonfiction readings, and used their resources both in and out of the classroom. The readings allowed students to meaningfully engage in knowledge-building discourse through what we define as the Nonfiction Text Science Learning Cycle. Next is a description of the phases in the Nonfiction Text Science Learning Cycle.

Introduction. The first phase of the Nonfiction Text Science Learning Cycle is the Introduction. During this time, teachers present students with short, nonfiction science readings to introduce, or launch, the topic of the lesson or unit. As students read, the teachers engage them in metacognitive questioning practices, where students are asked questions such as, "What surprised you?" "What did I already know about that topic?" and "What changed about what I thought I knew?" During this point of the cycle, the texts function as purveyors of information that may challenge students' assumptions.

Christine gave an example of when students' assumptions about the fur color of foxes was challenged by a reading: "That concept for them, that their fur color can change to adapt to their environment, was, like, 'How do they change colors?' Learning about the different adaptations, they know things, but I don't think they've ever really thought about why."

Another way in which these teachers invite students into the topic is through a series of statements. The students use these statements to make public their knowledge or initial wonderings about a topic. The teachers use these students' thinkings as a preassessment as they explore preexisting knowledge, assumptions, and misunderstandings about a topic. The introduction discussions, either initiated by a short nonfiction reading or a discussion based on statements, led into the next phase of the cycle—Investigation.

Investigation. During the Investigation phase of the Nonfiction Text Science Learning Cycle, students engage in scientific practices to make observations, gather evidence, and test their hypotheses. In all scientific investigations, students first state a claim. They then have to provide data to test their claims. Then they need to provide a reason the data happens, which is where the connection to nonfiction texts plays a role. Students can again explore their readings from the Introduction phase, or other nonfiction texts, to interpret or explain their findings. During the Investigation phase, the texts operate as a comparative resource for students' own scientific laboratory findings.

However, not all investigations are based on hands-on exploration. Sometimes students read nonfiction texts, such as online scientific research articles and STEMscopes readings, and then engage in small-group or whole-group discussions for the entire class period to construct and challenge their knowledge. Although students may be disappointed when they do not get to perform hands-on laboratory activities, Christine explains to her students that reading and discussion are still part of the job of people in science careers: "That's part of science, too. You have to read that nonfiction and get that knowledge. [The students] still have fun with it, it seems." This enjoyment can lead to the next stage of the cycle—Extension.

Extension. During the Extension phase of the Nonfiction Text Science Learning Cycle, students may research and explore additional texts because they are invested in their own learning and want to continue the learning process outside of the classroom. Patty shared an anecdote about students' furthering their scientific learning: "It's very common for them to come in and tell us that they found a book about what we're studying in here."

The information they find may provide scientific information that critically questions or supports their own findings from their lab. Because of this, some students come to class already knowing the content. During one of Christine's lessons, one boy recently took part in the Extension phase of the cycle, and he said, "'Everything you're talking about, I know about, or I've read about.' He raised his hand like three or four times and said, 'I read this book that said . . . .'"

Not only were students extending content learning to their homes, but they also became invested in nonfiction science texts. Christine explained, "When

I was in school, it wasn't cool to read nonfiction. And now I see these kids, their books that they're reading are nonfiction books. They're excited about nonfiction texts that we read in science. They're into it now . . . They want to know, 'What can I do to help [with real problems]?'" Patty confirmed and believed that "kids just really want to read about what's real. They just want to know facts. . . . They want to know about life."

The teachers were surprised that students took it upon themselves to find additional, nonfiction information related to their classroom learning. In other words, these young people were making public their (nonfiction) reading as well as their learning. This inquisitive energy may have occurred in part because the teachers had modified their teaching philosophies to explain to students that they would not give them the right answer—sometimes there was not a right answer to give.

Christine explained, "Sometimes when you tell them you're not going to give them the right answer, it's like: 'What? Why aren't you going to tell me what the answer is? That's why I'm here. I'm trying to get this information.' And we have to explain that we want you to find out the information. If you find it for yourself, it's going to stick with you." That learning of new information is exactly what the students were doing. Some of them bring the resources they find back to class with them, where they take part in the next phase of the cycle—Propulsion.

Propulsion. During the Propulsion phase of the Nonfiction Text Science Learning Cycle, the students use their discovered resources as fuel for propelling their own learning back in the classroom. Some students use their resources to propose additional questions and learning activities, such as watching supporting videos and discussing them as a class. Students may also use their resources to critique and clarify their understanding of the scientific topics. In this sense, students could use their own nonfiction texts to compare and contrast information with their laboratory findings, their classroom readings, and the teachers' statements.

The teachers indicated that the students found related nonfiction books that they used to question teachers' knowledge; essentially, the texts allow students to engage in the process of generating science truth by empowering them to challenge the knowledge of authority. Students learn that the hierarchy of scientific knowledge may be collapsed when the power of knowledge ownership is provided to them.

Patty explained:

One young man in fifth grade that you wouldn't think would be interested in science—he's really cool. When we were doing our STEMscope, and we were reading about the stars and constellations, every day he came, he had his own personal book about the stars. This big old book, brought it every day to class. Everything we were talking about, he was looking it up in the book to see if it's right. Some kids that you just wouldn't think would be turned on to things like earth systems. He can look it up to just verify that everything that I'm teaching is right.

Christine also gave an example of students who engaged in the Propulsion stage. She remarks:

Two in particular, when we were doing our star stuff, she would leave me notes like, "Check out this . . . it's a really cool video about the size of planets." I had this girl who was going home and was looking up things on YouTube so she could come in and be like, "Guess what I found." I had another little boy who would go home and he always wanted to catch me in something. He would go home and research stuff and bring it in and say, "This is the information that I found."

Finally she gave in and showed the video and looked at the resources, and discovered they were great starting points for a discussion. She followed up, "They were bringing lessons to me to be able to teach them."

Our participants, Patty and Christine, celebrated their students' empowerment to take their learning outside of the classroom. They acknowledged that some students who were not typically engaged in the regular classroom have found new enthusiasm for learning. Students were no longer third, fourth, or fifth grade students; they were now scientists who question; hypothesize; experiment; record, organize, and analyze data; make conclusions; observe; classify; compare; measure; predict; infer; communicate; estimate; practice safety skills; and make models.

The Nonfiction Text Science Learning Cycle provided students an opportunity to authentically engage with scientific truth, similar to how scientists do. (See figure 6.1.)

The texts scaffolded the students' learning throughout this cycle, helping to introduce, investigate, extend, and propel scientific learning. The vital aspect of this cycle was that students learned to check, challenge, and question not only their own knowledge, but also the knowledge of the authority figures—the teachers. They made the choice to engage with the texts—it was a desire to continue learning that motivated them to find, read, and critique additional resources.

If students found informational discrepancies or used their resources to pursue another avenue of learning, they could continue the cycle to the Introduction point and begin again. We feel that each time students rotate

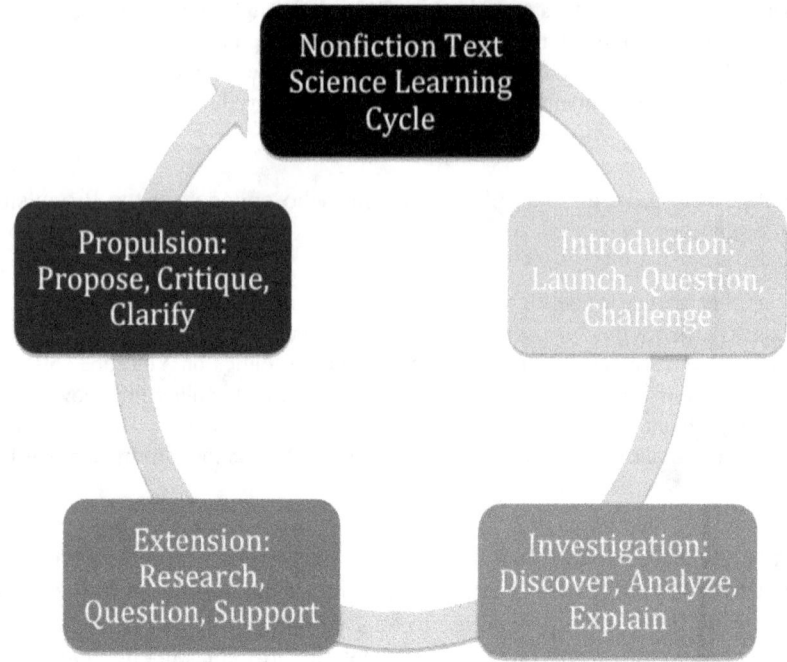

Figure 6.1.   The Nonfiction Text Science Learning Cycle. *Source*: Shanetia Clark and Vincent Genareo.

through this cycle, they may get closer to discovering the complexities of scientific knowledge. Perhaps understanding the complexity and nuances of testing, developing, and refining knowledge is an accurate definition of *scientific truth*.

CONCLUSION

The Nonfiction Text Science Learning Cycle demonstrates what an active and engaged science lab (classroom) could look like. We have found that this cycle epitomizes classroom teachers' and students' reciprocal colearning relationship. In addition to physical experiments, the use of nonfiction texts such as journal and news articles, trade books, and websites ignites a curiosity in students' learning. This cycle enables students, as well as teachers, to move beyond the traditional classroom textbook-based instruction and promotes the texts as tools for authentically introducing, exploring, challenging, and reinforcing students' views of scientific truth.

NOTES

1. To protect the identity of the school and the school district, pseudonyms are being used.

2. The statistical information regarding the demographic data for this district detailed in tables 6.1 to 6.4 was retrieved from the 2016 Maryland Report Card, Maryland State Department of Education (2017).

3. In order to protect the identity of the participants, pseudonyms are being used.

4. See the National Science Teachers Association's Outstanding Science Trade Books that are recognized each year. For more information about the selected list, visit this website: http://www.nsta.org/publications/ostb/.

REFERENCES

Accelerated Learning. (2017). Introducing STEMscopes. Retrieved from https://www.acceleratelearning.com/.

Coleman, J. M., & Dantzler, J. A. (2016). The frequency and type of graphical representations in science trade books for children. *Journal of Visual Literacy*, *35*(1), 24–41.

Creswell, J. W. (2018). *Qualitative inquiry and research design: Choosing among five approaches.* 4th edition. Thousand Oaks, CA: Sage.

Doiron, R. (1994). Using nonfiction in a read-aloud program: Letting the facts speak for themselves. *The Reading Teacher, 47*, 616–624.

Ford, D. J. (2006). Representations of science within children's trade books. *Journal of Research in Science Teaching, 43*(2), 214–235.

Gill, S. R. (2009). What teachers need to know about the "new" nonfiction. *The Reading Teacher, 63*(4), 260–267.

Hammer, D. (1995). Epistemological considerations in teaching introductory physics. *Science Education, 79*(4), 393–413.

James, S. (1991). *Dear Mr. Blueberry*. New York, NY: Maxwell Macmillan International.

Job, J., & Coleman, M. R. (2016). The importance of reading in earnest: Non-fiction for young children. *Gifted Child Today, 39*(3), 154–163.

Kiefer, B. Z., & Tyson, C. A. (2013). *Charlotte Huck's children's literature: A brief guide* (2nd ed.). New York, NY: McGraw-Hill.

Klosterman, C. (2016). *But what if we're wrong?* New York, NY: Penguin Random House LLC.

Krajcik, J., Codere, S., Dahsah, C., Bayer, R., & Mun, K. (2014). Planning instruction to meet the intent of the Next Generation Science Standards. *Journal of Science Teacher Education, 25*(2), 157–175.

Maryland State Department of Education. (2017). *2016 Maryland report card*. Retrieved from http://reportcard.msde.maryland.gov/.

Mayer, D.A. (1995). How can we best use children's literature in teaching science concepts? *Science and Children, 32*(6), 16–19.

National Science Teachers Association. (2017). *Outstanding science trade books for students K–12*. Retrieved from http://www.nsta.org/publications/ostb/.

NGSS Release (2013). *Appendix F—Science and engineering practices in the NGSS*. Retrieved from http://www.nextgenscience.org/sites/default/files/Appendix%20 F%20%20Science%20and%20Engineering%20Practices%20in%20the%20 NGSS%20-%20FINAL%20060513.pdf.

Rice, D. C. (2002). Using trade books in teaching elementary science: Facts and fallacies. *The Reading Teacher, 55*(6), 552–565.

Tsai, C. C. (1999). "Laboratory exercises help me memorize the scientific truths": A study of eighth graders' scientific epistemological views and learning in laboratory activities. *Science Education, 83*(6), 654–674.

Waters, H. (2011). Why scientists should read science fiction. Retrieved from https://blogs.scientificamerican.com/culturing-science/why-scientists-should-read-science-fiction/.

Chapter Seven

Engaging Young Adolescents through Science

L. J. Phillips and Marnie Woodley

From the time they can talk, children ask questions. They want to know how wheels turn, why ducks float, why the sky is blue. They try things and see what happens, learning from their observations and then trying things differently. It may be a block that doesn't fit in the hole a particular way or a snow fort that collapses or a stream that needs crossing. This innate curiosity is a trait found in most successful people, who tend to be generalists and curious about everything.

They gather information and sift through it pondering the connections. Indeed, it is said that as a boy Albert Einstein was discovered by his mother lying awake at night, staring at the ceiling. When she asked him why he couldn't sleep he responded that he was thinking about where the light went after she turned it out (Harvey, 1998, loc. 312). Einstein never stopped being curious, and Jessica Berne's biographical picture book, *On a Beam of Light*, recounts how a sixteen-year-old Einstein wondered what it would be like to ride a beam of light. His continual questioning and research resulted in his famous theory of relativity.

On a Beam of Light presents readers with a young Einstein; a boy who didn't want to be like everyone else. He was a boy who questioned everything and grew into a man who questioned everything. Einstein's contribution to the world of science is a testament to curiosity, and he once claimed,

the most important thing is not to stop questioning. Curiosity has its own reason for existing. One cannot help but be in awe when he contemplates the mysteries of eternity, of life, of the marvellous structure of reality. It is enough if one tries merely to comprehend a little of this mystery every day. Never lose a holy curiosity. (Einstein quoted by Del Turco, 2017)

Yet at some point many children stop questioning. Do they stop wondering or do they just keep their wondering to themselves? Are they just reacting to repeated pleas from adults to be quiet, to listen and to stop asking so many questions? It's no secret that scientific discovery comes from those who need to solve a problem, figure out a better way to make something work, or wonder "what if."

Today's child is growing up in a different world, yet they begin just as curious as a young Albert Einstein. Einstein retreated into books to find his answers, reading everything he could get his hands on and answering questions with new questions (Berne, 2016). Maybe therein lies the answer. Throughout this chapter we demonstrate how teachers might nurture students' scientific curiosity through integrative thinking.

INTEGRATIVE THINKING AND LEARNING

During the integrative thinking process, students draw from every area of knowledge and propose solutions to a problem (i.e., how to get from what they have to what they want). The process is the focus of Roger Martin's book *The Opposable Mind: How Successful Leaders Win through Integrative Thinking*. Martin (2009) claims that leaders "have the predisposition and the capacity to hold two diametrically opposing ideas in their heads. And then, without panicking or simply settling for one alternative or the other, they're able to produce a synthesis that is superior to either opposing idea" (p. 6). He goes on to say that the upcoming generation must be able to look for new solutions "as success in the global economy depends on the ability to wade through ambiguous challenges, managing difficult trade-offs with flexibility and creativity" (p. 14).

Martin is the former dean of the Rotman School of Management at the University of Toronto, where the integrative thinking process has evolved into the I-Think program. The program is designed to challenge students with a "wicked" problem, one with unacceptable trade-offs. The process leads students to new and innovative solutions, as they research new questions and weigh up possibilities (Rotman I-Think program, 2015).

Martin's book focuses on the process as it applies to business leadership (see figure 7.1 for a summary of his four-step process) as does the Rotman School, but the process is valuable regardless of the topic of the "wicked" question. Through a partnership with the Toronto District School Board, the Rotman School has adapted the concepts to the high school level, asking students to consider all aspects of a problem, weigh ideas and difficulties from all constituents, and then develop a creative solution.

THINK OUTSIDE THE BOX

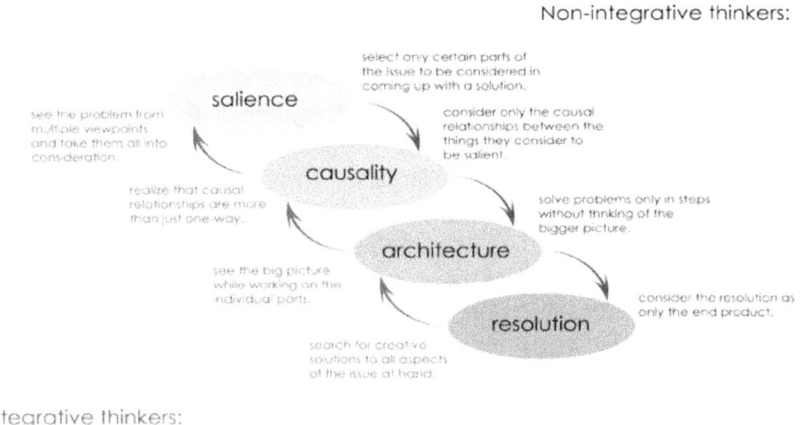

Figure 7.1. **Integrative Thinking.** *Source:* **Rotman's ithink program 2015.**

A group of grade twelve students at John Polanyi Collegiate Institute realized the current campaign against homophobia was not working. Rather than choose between options, they looked for new connections between those options and presented to their school a new way of thinking about homophobia and tolerance in general (Avishai, 2013).

As a unit or an independent study in integrative thinking, students can be presented with a challenging problem that requires them to draw from all areas of their knowledge to apply and investigate scientific applications in both the middle school and high school classroom.

TECHNOLOGY, DISCOVERY, AND INNOVATIVE LEARNING

With the exponential growth of technology, today's child is surrounded by information. Anything they might wonder is at their fingertips and just a Google search away. But this is knowledge that already exists. In the elementary classroom, leading questions like "What temperature must it be in order for it to snow?" are asked as students examine the world around them and learn what we already know. It's the unanswered questions that need to be explored. Nurturing children to continue to question and search for answers is vital as they can become complacent with the amount of easily accessible information. When a child asks a question, we should challenge them to find an answer, and often technology can assist with this task.

With the mandated focus on literacy and numeracy, cross-curricular lessons and exploration are even more important in ensuring the science curriculum is not shortchanged. In recent years, STEM (science, technology, engineering, and mathematics) subjects have begun to receive more attention, but standardized testing still emphasizes language and mathematics. *The Washington Post* reported in 2015 that "a typical student takes 112 mandated standardized tests between pre-kindergarten classes and 12th grade. . . . By contrast, most countries that outperform the United States on international exams test students three times during their school careers" (Layton, 2015).

This number may have decreased since the report, yet it is still alarmingly out of proportion in comparison. Test preparation can become a focus when testing occurs so frequently, drawing teachers away from creative learning in favor of getting students "through the test." This raises the possibility that students may be given the facts they need for the test rather than being allowed to *discover* the material during the learning process.

Despite the general acceptance that creativity is vital to discovery and innovation, it is not something that is easily measured on a standardized test. And there is not much in life that resembles a standardized test or any test for that matter. Employers aren't looking to hire the best test-taker; they want the idea person, the innovator who will patent a new idea. A 2010 IBM poll of 1,500 CEOs identified creativity as the number one leadership competency of the future (Hansen, 2012). So if this is the future, why is creativity still taking a backseat in the classroom?

We have entered a new Renaissance requiring connectivity and integration, and the education system is struggling to catch up. The technological age and the Internet have had a similar impact on society, as did the invention of the printing press. Easily accessible information produced by the printing press heralded the arrival of the Renaissance thinker, as more questions arose and new inventions were the result. The parallels to the twenty-first century are unmistakable, and this Renaissance (or polymath) mind is once again necessary for development.

According to psychologist Seymour Epstein, humans have two interacting thinking modes, the rational and the experiential. His research indicates the importance of tapping into both thinking modes and harnessing the positive aspects of each (Kaufman, 2011). In correspondence with *Psychology Today* journalist Scott Kaufman, Epstein clarified the resurgent need for the Renaissance thinker:

> people who are high in both thinking styles are Renaissance people. They have the brains of scientists and the sensibilities of poets. In other words they have the positive features of both thinking styles and do not have their negative features because they are kept under control by the other thinking style. (Kaufman, 2011)

Great thinkers draw from all areas of knowledge, and connectivity leads them to new discoveries, just as Einstein wondered about riding that beam of light.

INTEGRATIVE THINKING AND MIDDLE SCHOOL SCIENCE

So how do we nurture students in their quest for understanding when we are mired in testing? In Canada, we have a prescribed curriculum in the science classroom; however, how we get there is usually left up to the teacher. Our own classrooms are guided by integrative thinking, and a further look at middle school and high school science classrooms revealed a number of opportunities for integrative thinking.

Integrative thinking is not difficult in the elementary school classroom, where often teachers are teaching all subjects. Integration is also possible in the middle school classroom, where cross-curricular objectives often enter the curriculum.

Regardless of whether one is teaching all subjects in grades seven and eight or specifically teaching science, starting a unit by reading a particular text out loud provides many jumping-off points for integrative thinking and will provoke questions that can be explored during the unit. Introducing texts in a science-specific class also plants the idea that knowledge acquired in other classes is helpful for scientific discovery. You may even find that students are so surprised to be read to in science class, they are even more engaged as they try to figure out what the teacher is up to.

Kakapo Rescue by Sy Montgomery prompts many areas of exploration. It tells the story of a group of scientists and their quest to save a charming and almost extinct parrot on an island off the south coast of New Zealand. The book uses photographs rather than illustrations and includes a selected bibliography and direction to a web page devoted to the rescue program. The web page is updated daily, allowing students to follow the scientists' continuing work. The book is detailed and thus lengthy, but reading selections from it will be enough to raise questions of inquiry.

While the learning goal may be to examine the life cycle or biology of birds, students may develop an interest in New Zealand and wish to look at other animals there. They may want to find out more about what a botanist does or how the Kakapo makes such an unusual noise.

Give them access to the Internet and books, which will keep them immersed in their area of interest. If they are reading, they are developing literacy; if they are calculating extinction rates, they are developing numeracy; and if they are looking at bird songs, they are developing their understanding of biology. As of June 2017, there were 154 kakapos in the world, and the website provides pictures of specific kakapos available for "adoption" (Adopt a Kākāpō, 2015). Consider adopting a kakapo for your class and following the parrot's story. Regardless of where the inquiry takes your students, they won't be able to resist the allure of the charming bird and its fight for survival.

INTEGRATIVE THINKING AND HIGH SCHOOL SCIENCE

The challenge increases in the high school years when students begin to worry more about their grades, standardized testing, and getting into their preferred universities. It is a constant frustration for high school teachers, and universities continue to complain that students are not prepared for the "analytic and conceptual thinking they'll need at university" (Slavin, 2007).

So again, the problem becomes how might teachers allow students to follow their interests while still preparing them for examinations. Until the education system is reformed to keep up with the times, we are stuck with a delicate balancing act. All teachers want their students to revel in the excitement of discovery, yet we are hampered by an assigned curriculum.

While the temptation may be to err on the side of caution and stick with worksheets and tests, students can also demonstrate their understanding while being allowed to explore and develop the integrative thinking skills so sought after in university and thereafter. The key is in developing projects that give the students choices to pursue their interests.

While still being mindful of safety (we don't want exploding classrooms or escaping mice), let students try out the "what-ifs" they have been wondering about. Rather than giving them a prescribed experiment to conduct, let them make up one of their own. Have them write up their proposed ideas so you can be sure nothing will explode, and then provide them with the necessary support. Maybe they want to create a perfume or analyze the components of a lipstick. You may not be on optics yet, or body systems, or space flight, and it may prove to be a logistical challenge, but letting students create their own scientific exploration will make them invested in finding out what happens. Allowing students to design the class rather than being told what they will be doing and how they will be doing it, will give them ownership and in turn an investment in their learning.

With the amount of curriculum that needs to be covered in the high school science classroom, literacy takes on a different dimension, for students must be able to communicate in scientific language. They need to learn concise writing and communication of their discoveries just like they do in every other subject. Nonfiction texts should be presented as examples of scientific writing allowing students to become familiar with report formats and the scientific writer's voice. Present them with research papers and journal articles as background reading. You may be surprised by how much they absorb that will expand their vocabulary and translate into their own writing.

While a course based on integrative thinking can be challenging with so many specific expectations and objectives to be ticked off, it is even more necessary in the high school classroom as students prepare for higher learning. Plan an integrative unit or develop an independent study project that allows students to choose their field of inquiry. It should be a unit devoted to the process rather than assessment.

Creative nonfiction texts are a natural fit with this sort of unit. Have students bring in a nonfiction text they'd like to explore further. Encourage them to think about something they want to investigate and then research texts in that field. The more wide-open the process, the more likely the student is to enjoy an extended project. Some students may want to read together like in a literature circle, which could prompt even more discussion in that field.

Bomb by Steve Sheinkin is an excellent example of a text that can be used with all students, even those who may not enjoy reading and may wonder why science class is suddenly "English" class. *Bomb* is the story of Oppenheimer's Manhattan project and the race to build the first nuclear weapon during the Second World War. It reads like a spy novel while explaining the physics behind the bomb with great clarity.

A group of scientists gather secretly in Los Alamos and are presented with a problem: "produce a practical military weapon in the form of a bomb in which the energy is released by a fast-neutron chain reaction" (Sheinkin, chapter 17). The story is an excellent example of the integrative thinking process and the pressure to perform. Oppenheimer's group of scientists were presented with a seemingly impossible problem and tasked with solving it—a challenge in integrative thinking.

In your own classroom, you could present students with the "wicked" problem of how to build a boat that will carry two people one hundred meters. Not an insurmountable problem but difficult because of the number of decisions to be made. If time is limited, add limitations to narrow the possibilities like, the boat must be constructed from the provided cardboard and duct tape. Students look at the two seemingly insurmountable problems of the permeable nature of the material (cardboard) and the added weight of two students.

Give them each a small journal and encourage them to write down all the questions that needed answering. Encourage them to draw ideas, jot down musings and take notes creating a pattern of the thought process much as Leonardo Da Vinci did in his journals (see figure 7.2).

OF THE SEA, WHICH TO MANY FOOLS APPEARS TO BE HIGHER THAN THE EARTH WHICH FORMS ITS SHORE.

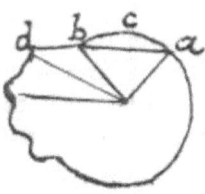

b d is a plain through which a river flows to the sea; this plain ends at the sea, and since in fact the dry land that is uncovered is not perfectly level--for, if it were, the river would have no motion--as the river does move, this place is a slope rather than a plain; hence this plain *d b* so ends where the sphere of water begins that if it were extended in a continuous line to *b a* it would go down beneath the sea, whence it follows that the sea *a c b* looks higher than the dry land. Obviously no portions of dry land left uncovered by water can ever be lower than the surface of the watery sphere.

Figure 7.2.   Example from Da Vinci's Notebooks. *Source*: Da Vinci's Notebooks

One of the greatest Renaissance thinkers, Da Vinci was as well known for his scientific thinking as he was for his art. Da Vinci never lost his curiosity, and his journals are an example of an intriguing mind at work. Reading excerpts from these journals (Richter, 1883) is a good starting point for the project. Allow students to jot down questions as they listen and then explore their questions further either through discussion or research.

Their questions may not be what you're looking for or the direction you'd like them to follow, but allow them to spend as much time as possible learning about the value of musing, and wondering. Encourage them to write down anything and everything in their journals and remind them that you never know what idea will take you in a new direction.

Once students are presented with the initial question of how to make cardboard carry two people, they will continue to write in their journals. Try to refrain from giving direction in this area. You'll find that they will begin to make lists and doodle ideas. They will look at the problems and write down questions they need to solve. Eventually, they will discover that they need to use Archimedes' principle to start. This may be something they already know, or something they have to look up or ask about.

Smartphones can be useful tools for finding answers, but you'll have to decide how much you're going to allow them to be distracted by the phones and as such get off topic. Once the questions start rolling, they may find themselves looking up answers to questions that have arisen but don't actually help with the task; however, this is when it becomes more about the process than the actual end product. The project can also be run on a smaller scale where students build a cardboard boat and then see how much weight it can hold.

The competition element of the boat challenge often heightens student investment in the inquiry and keeps them on track when time is an issue; however, winning rather than learning could take over the project, so be mindful about this. Alternatively, leave the build project open-ended and allow them to build or investigate whatever they like. Allow them to work together or alone if they prefer.

If students are able to focus on the discovery and the integrative thinking process rather than having particular objectives that need to be fulfilled, you will find more engagement and enthusiasm for this sort of unit. They could research needs within the school or the local neighborhood. They may want to work with a charity. It *is* a fine balance between allowing their curiosity to take over while still giving them some direction, but the engagement will be greater.

Given more time and resources, robot building is another opportunity for integrative thinking. Students design and build a robot to complete a certain task. Similar to the boat-building process, they weigh up the goals and the obstacles to reaching the goal. If you're looking for a prompt to lead into the project, *Almost Human: Making Robots Think* by Lee Gutkind (2009) describes the world of robotics and roboticists and puts readers in the moment with the frustration and celebrations of the creative process, much like Sheinkin's (2012) *Bomb: The Race to Build—and Steal—the World's Most Dangerous Weapon*. The novel prompts inquiry about mechanics and physics while also raising questions around artificial intelligence and what makes us human.

As in the boat challenge, have students jot down questions in their Da Vinci journals and consider possible answers. You can then decide where you want them to go with any kind of creation. You can let them loose with the entire Lego bin or with a specific list of materials, or you can give them a challenge or focus. If you find the interest is there, you could consider a larger project, maybe moving outside the classroom and allowing students more time to solve a problem.

The First Robotics program and the Marine Advanced Technology Education (MATE) competition challenge teams to build a robot to accomplish a specific task. Points are given for accomplishing the task within a certain time limit. The robot may be required to shoot a basket while preventing an opponent from doing the same. Or it may be tasked with gathering "trash" from the bottom of a swimming pool. Teams work together to deconstruct the challenge and anticipate problems. Both competitions also require elements of marketing and sportsmanship, challenging teams to weigh up the strengths of their team members in a variety of areas.

These sorts of programs fit well as a stand-alone course or a yearlong extracurricular project. The time commitment is heavy, and the forced rules of competition may or may not be a draw for students. Regardless, the length of the challenges allows for creativity in the planning process and true

Table 7.1. Texts to Prompt Inquiry in the Middle and High School Classroom

Text	Discovery Angle of Focus
Wicked Plants: The Weed That Killed Lincoln's Mother and Other Botanical Atrocities by Amy Stewart, Briony Morrow-Cribbs	Botany
The Disappearing Spoon: And Other True Tales of Madness, Love, and the History of the World from the Periodic Table of the Elements by Sam Kean	The periodic table
The World Without Us by Alan Weisman	Environment/ecology
Where the Germs Are: A Scientific Safari by Nicholas Bakalar	Microbiology
What If? Serious Scientific Answers to Absurd Hypothetical Questions by Randall Munroe	Scientific process
The Selfish Gene by Richard Dawkins	Genetics/evolution
The Story of the Human Body: Evolution, Health and Disease by Daniel Lieberman	Evolution
Patient Zero: Solving the Mysteries of Deadly Epidemics by Marilee Peter	Epidemiology
The Human Microbiome: The Germs That Keep You Healthy by Rebecca E. Hirsch	Microbiology
Bad Science by Ben Goldacre	Scientific process
Physics of the Future: How Science Will Shape Human Destiny and Our Daily Lives by the Year 2100 by Michio Kaku	Physics/careers in science
Slow Light: Invisibility, Teleportation and Other Mysteries of Light by Sidney Perkowitz	Physics
The Physics of Superheroes by James Kakalios	Physics
Last Chance to See by Douglas Adams, Mark Carwardine	Environment/diversity/ extinction
Periodic Tales: The Curious Lives of the Elements by Hugh Aldersey-Williams	The periodic table
Bomb by Steve Sheinkin	Physics
Kakapo Rescue: Saving the World's Strangest Parrot by Sy Montgomery	Environment
Almost Human by Lee Gutkind	Robotics

integrative thinking as the students work together to build the robot, very much like Oppenheimer's team worked together to solve their challenge in a specific time period.

Educators in the twenty-first century face more challenges than ever before. A rapidly evolving workplace means we are preparing students for jobs that don't exist. We have a curriculum to follow and students who are concerned about their grades rather than their learning. Creativity is valued in tomorrow's leaders, yet more and more society is suffocating children, structuring every minute of their day and telling them how to behave.

Risk management has curtailed many programs, and outdoor play areas are vanishing. Children are left with little time for pause and wonder. Children must be allowed to discover on their own, to wonder and consider "what if?" Nurturing a child's natural curiosity prompts a lifelong love of learning. Allow your students to ride their own beam of light. You never know where it might take them.

REFERENCES

Adopt a Kākāpō. (2015). Retrieved June 4, 2017, from http://kakaporecovery.org.nz /adopt-a-kakapo/.

Avishai, E. (November 2013). Cultivating an opposable mind: A case study in integrative thinking. Education Canada. Retrieved June 12, 2017, from http://www .cea-ace.ca/education-canada/article/cultivating-opposable-mind.

Del Turco, Brian (2017). Einstein said, "Never lose a holy curiosity." Retrieved May 31, 2017, from http://www.truenorthquest.com/einstein-never-lose-holy-curiosity/. Originally published in "Death of a genius," *Life*, May 2, 1955.

FIRST Robotics Competition. (April 23, 2017). Retrieved June 4, 2017, from https:// www.firstinspires.org/robotics/frc.

Gutkind, L. (2009). *Almost human: Making robots think.* New York, NY: W. W. Norton & Co.

Hansen, D. (2012). Steve Jobs isn't the only kind of artist leader. Retrieved June 4, 2017, from https://www.forbes.com/sites/drewhansen/2012/12/29/steve-jobs-isnt-the-only-kind-of-artist-leader/#4d4866374345.

Harvey, S. (1998). *Nonfiction matters: Reading, writing, and research in grades 3-8* [Kindle version].

Kaufman, S. B. (2011). How Renaissance people think. Retrieved June 4, 2017, from https://www.psychologytoday.com/blog/beautiful-minds/201106/how-renaissance-people-think.

Layton, L. (2015). Study says standardized testing is overwhelming nation's public schools. Retrieved May 31, 2017, from https://www.washingtonpost.com/ local/education/study-says-standardized-testing-is-overwhelming-nations

-public schools/2015/10/24/8a22092c-79ae-11e5-a958-d889faf561dc_story .html?utm_term=.252e8bfab6fb.

Marine Advanced Technology Education: ROV Competition Home. (2012). Retrieved June 4, 2017, from https://www.marinetech.org/rov-competition-2/.

Martin, R. L. (2009). *The opposable mind: How successful leaders win through integrative thinking.* Boston, MA: Harvard Business School Press.

Richter, J. P. (Ed.). (1883). The Notebooks of Leonardo Da Vinci. Retrieved June 4, 2017, from http://sacred-texts.com/aor/dv/index.htm.

Rier, J. (2013). Successful transition to proficiency-based diploma starts now. Retrieved June 4, 2017, from https://mainedoenews.net/2013/10/17/successful-transition-to-proficiency-based-diploma-starts-now/.

Rotman I-Think Program teaches students to think like leaders. (April 1, 2015). Retrieved June 4, 2017, from https://www.teachontario.ca/community/explore/teachontario-talks/blog/2015/04/01/i-think-program-teaches-students-to-think-like-business-leaders.

Slavin, A. (2007). Has Ontario taught its high-school students not to think? Retrieved June 4, 2017, from http://www.universityaffairs.ca/opinion/in-my-opinion/has-ontario-taught-its-high-school-students-not-to-think/.

Think outside the box [Online image]. (2013). Retrieved June 12, 2017 from https://www.hunchmanifest.com/category/innovation/.

CHILDREN'S BOOKS CITED

Berne, J., & Radunsky, V. (2016). *On a beam of light: A story of Albert Einstein.* San Francisco, CA: Chronicle Books LLC.

Montgomery, S. (2016). *Kakapo rescue: Saving the world's strangest parrot.* New York, NY: Houghton Mifflin Harcourt.

Sheinkin, S. (2012). *Bomb: The race to build—and steal—the world's most dangerous weapon.* New York, NY: Flash Point.

Chapter Eight

Engaging Students in Conversations about "Mathematical Truths"

Deanna Day and Barbara A. Ward

While mathematics and nonfiction might seem like an unlikely partnership, just as some educators have found value in combining mathematics with children's fiction, teachers have come to recognize that the two actually work well together. In this chapter, we seek to understand the importance of identifying and integrating quality nonfiction in math instruction. This chapter critically explores recent nonfiction texts with possible mathematical connections and suggests some useful nonfiction titles for primary and intermediate grades.

In addition, the chapter examines the perspectives of preservice teachers on current math nonfiction and suggests ways that children's nonfiction can be used to teach math concepts or mathematical truths. Furthermore, we share how students can engage in conversations about mathematics books, and highlight a classroom teacher who integrates math literature into her instruction. Lastly, the chapter includes a list of current math titles and explores some "mathematical truths" that exist in nonfiction texts for children.

WHY LITERATURE?

Often elementary school teachers tend to separate subject areas when they are teaching, reserving certain amounts of time for specific parts of the curriculum, thus dividing the instructional day into discrete units devoted to reading, writing, or mathematics. But this approach might not be ideal since it tends to lead students to regard various content areas and subjects as being separate, while failing to honor the possibilities various disciplines offer for literacy instruction, and how literacy instruction offers potential to explore math from a real-world perspective.

Since children's literature provides actual global problems that encourage students to draw on their funds of knowledge to solve various math problems, children's trade books offer some of the best places to marry these subjects (Lake, 2009; McDuffie, Young, & Ward, in press). Austin (1998) cautions teachers to avoid focusing so heavily on mathematics that books lose their appeal as literature for young readers in favor of a lesson that is being taught. After all, the joy of reading for pleasure and information should always be at the forefront when using any children's trade books with young readers.

At this point, it might be helpful to pause for a moment and consider whether classroom teachers should or shouldn't use children's literature during math instruction. Have you used or witnessed a teacher using children's literature during math instruction? Take a moment and ponder this question.

Columba, Kim, and Moe (2005) and McDuffie and Young (2003) state teachers should use children's literature as part of math lessons because it:

- Humanizes math in the eyes of children and parents
- Challenges the stereotypes of math as sterile, noncreative, or unrelated to life
- Builds on the positive reactions children have to reading stories
- Integrates learning in a variety of disciplines
- Provides an alternative medium for learning about math
- Stimulates children's math interest, enjoyment, and confidence

How do these researchers' viewpoints on integrating children's literature compare to your thoughts and feelings about literature in math instruction?

The coauthors asked preservice students in a math methods course the same question as to whether they thought children's literature should be used to teach math. Although at first they were a bit surprised by the question, they overwhelmingly saw value in doing so. Through a math nonfiction picture book, teachers can figure out their students' prior knowledge about math concepts or topics. Read-alouds of math books might also be a formative assessment where teachers gain an idea of what math concepts they may need to teach. Furthermore, math literature introduces math vocabulary in a different way than the approach in most math texts since vocabulary is embedded within real-life examples and relatable scenarios.

In another literacy methods course, future elementary and middle grade students were given the chance to browse through an extensive collection of math books. One student was surprised that most of the recent publications featured individuals who used math to work with computers. "I always thought that they were separate. I didn't think that writing code for computer programs or software was related to math, but of course it is."

After exploring a plethora of math-related concept books by David A. Adler (see table 8.1), who is adept at demystifying some of the more confus-

Table 8.1.   David A. Adler Math Books

Let's Estimate: A Book about Estimating and Rounding Numbers (2017)
Place Value (2016)
Circles (2016)
Fraction Fun (1996)
Fractions, Decimals, and Percents (2010)
Fun with Roman Numerals (2008)
Millions, Billions, and Trillions (2013)
Money Math (2017)
Mystery Math: A First Book of Algebra (2011)
Perimeter, Area, and Volume: A Monster Book of Dimensions (2012)
Shape Up: Fun with Triangles and Other Polygons (1998)
Triangles (2014)
Working with Fractions (2007)
You Can, Toucan, Math (2006)

ing aspects of math, including related but different terms such as *rounding* and *estimating*, another student with an admitted fear of math proclaimed, "Where were these books when I was younger? If I had read these books, I might have understood what my teachers were trying to say."

The preservice teachers also couldn't stop reading and smiling at how math concepts were taught in several books by Laura Overdeck, whose Bedtime Math titles include math riddles and mathematical problems. Overdeck's intention is to make math as much a part of a nightly bedtime ritual as reading picture books or chapter books. "I like how these books contain problems that are pitched to different audiences," said one student. "They'd be great for differentiated instruction since there is a problem geared to preschoolers but others in the same vein that are for high schoolers."

Some teachers themselves have a math phobia because they don't consider their own math skills to be very strong. This anxiety leads them to rely primarily on the scripted math curriculum provided by many school districts. But exploring math biographies and informational math texts with their students could benefit them and enhance their own knowledge as well as that of their students.

For instance, as anyone who has ever had to multiply a number with decimals or complete a tax form knows, place value is a simple but important math concept. Adler's picture book, *Place Value* (2016) introduces this concept in simple fashion, starting with the most basic idea and increasing in complexity in the later pages.

Another student was particularly taken by Adler's *Let's Estimate* (2017), which demonstrates the difference between rounding and estimating. "I always wondered how anyone could possibly count the number of indi-

viduals present at a concert or a public event," she said. "And now, thanks
to this trade book, one for kids, I now know. I guess it's never too late
to get excited about math." If a young adult can learn something about a
mathematical concept in an easy-to-digest fashion, it stands to reason that
younger students might profit from exploring these important aspects of
math in the same way.

As these students and other preservice teachers have come to realize, children's literature provides a helpful avenue through which to positively think
about numbers, math facts, and problem solving. There are children's and
young adult trade books to solidify math concepts such as geometry, fractions, and proportions. Every genre is represented in math literature, although
this chapter's focus is on nonfiction.

NONFICTION MATH BOOKS

Nonfiction books are referred to as the literature of fact since they convey
factual information about the world. Temple, Martinez, and Yokota (2014)
suggest that a good nonfiction book can also be classified as an informational
book because many writers prefer not to refer to their work as nonfiction
since doing so identifies their genre by what it *isn't*, rather than what it *is*.
Throughout this chapter we will use *informational books* and *nonfiction
books* interchangeably. Many teachers recognize that good informational
texts will hook a child's attention with a colorful cover or a catchy title and
then draw them in by deepening their curiosity about mathematics.

Informational math books give students access to important useful
information with facts, documented material, and sources. Informational
books are typically arranged by key concepts, main ideas, or distinguishing
characteristics and formatted in a particular way by presenting information
in a more general way to a specific one, from simple to more complex, and
from known information to unknown information. Naturally, the best nonfiction books are written in a conversational style that makes their ideas
easy to understand.

Before using informational or nonfiction math books in our classrooms
teachers should teach the text structures of nonfiction books to guide readers and mathematicians (see box 8.1). For example, before reading aloud the
picture book *Tiger Math: Learning to Graph from a Baby Tiger* (Nagda &
Bickel, 2000), a teacher could strategically place sticky notes to showcase the
different text structures and refer to an anchor poster that is displayed in the
classroom as they read aloud the book to their students. In addition, these text

Box 8.1.

Nonfiction Text Structures

- Description—The author gives descriptive characteristics to the topic.
- Chronological sequence—The author lists items usually in order, chronologically or numerically.
- Comparison/contrast—The author juxtaposes two or more entries and lists their similarities and differences.
- Cause and effect—The author states an action and then shows the effect or result of this action.
- Problem and solution—The author states a problem and then there is a solution.
- Graphics—Photographs, paintings, drawings, charts, maps, and copies of documents are included.
- Format—Included in the text are an index, glossary, table of contents, additional facts, reference list, and acknowledgment of experts. (Temple, Martinez & Yokota, 2014)

structures could be put on a bookmark to encourage students to notice them as they read informational titles.

It is worth noting that there are many more fiction trade books that mention math than informational texts related to math. Although there are no statistics bearing out this assertion, even a cursory examination of a bookstore and library shelves will attest to its accuracy. The dearth of nonfiction books about math might relate to how challenging it can be to write engaging books that introduce mathematical concepts without insulting readers or mimicking dry textbooks. By the same count, there are more picture-book biographies featuring scientists than mathematicians.

Various types of nonfiction picture books provide wonderful vehicles to dispel the myth that math is dull, unimaginative, or inaccessible (Burns, 2010). Children's literature can spark students' mathematical imaginations in ways that textbooks and workbooks cannot. Picture books also may help avid readers who think math isn't their favorite subject to find the same joy with math as they do with reading (Burns, 2010). Using picture books as a starting point for conversations about math or to begin a math lesson can become an effective technique, especially if this approach is handled similarly to reader's workshop.

At the beginning of reader's workshop teachers often share one-to-three-minute book talks to entice children or adolescents to "pick up a title" during silent or partner reading. Teachers often book-talk many fiction titles but need to book-talk nonfiction math texts as well. As many experts (Layne, 2009; Miller, 2009; Tunnell, Jacobs, Young, & Bryan, 2015) maintain, students often gravitate to the titles their teachers have just shared in class in the same way a movie trailer entices moviegoers to buy tickets for an upcoming film. Additionally, teachers can read aloud math books during read-aloud time or at the beginning of math instruction.

Griffiths and Clyne (1988) suggest combining mathematics and literature, used in conjunction with opportunities for talk and discussion, because this allows children to grapple with mathematical concepts in a meaningful context rather than encountering the concepts in isolation. After reading aloud a math book, teachers can invite students to share their thoughts about the books by asking, "What do you think?" "How do you feel?" "What connections do you have?" and "What mathematical truths did you notice?"

Table 8.2 contains a list of nonfiction math titles that could be read aloud or book-talked in elementary or middle school to highlight basic mathematical truths. We define "mathematical truths" as inquiries, themes, or concepts for teaching mathematics in K-12 classrooms.

Table 8.2.   Nonfiction Math Books

Title and author	Mathematical truths
Tiger Math: Learning to Graph from a Baby Tiger (Nagda & Bickel, 2000)	Graphing
Polar Bear Math: Learning about Fractions from Klondike and Snow (Nagda & Bickel, 2004)	Fractions
Cheetah Math: Learning about Division from Cheetahs (Nagda & Bickel, 2007)	Division
Panda Math: Learning about Subtraction from Hua Mei and Mei Sheng (Nagda, 2000)	Subtraction
Chimp Math: Learning about Time from a Baby Chimpanzee (Nagda & Bickel, 2002)	Time
Math Doesn't Suck: How to Survive Middle School Math without Losing Your Mind and Breaking a Nail (McKellar, 2008)	Fractions, percentages, prealgebra, and more
The History of Counting (Schmandt-Besserat, 1999)	Numbers
The History of Money: From Bartering to Banking (Jenkins, 2014)	Money, interest, taxes, and more

MATH BIOGRAPHIES

Temple, Martinez, and Yokota (2014) state that biographies are children's or adolescent works that describe and discuss the lives of real individuals. In recent years, a number of biographies about mathematicians have been published. Quality biographies need to inspire and interest readers, balance the individual's life, be accurate and authentic, have a writing style that is easy to read, and include a reference list.

One such title is *The Boy Who Loved Math: The Impossible Life of Paul Erdos* (Heiligman, 2013), which was an Orbis Pictus and Notable Children's Books for Language Arts winner. Even as a child, Paul Erdos loved playing with numbers and didn't like to follow rules. In fact, he disliked school and invented his own way to live. Since the detailed illustrations by LeUyen Pham incorporate math concepts, students might complete a scavenger hunt in which they identify what concepts the illustrator has woven into the book's images. Later, after discussing what they have found, they could work in pairs to find similar math concepts at work in their school and home community, sharing them in class the next day.

Reading and discussing math biographies enhance and expand children's conception of math and alter their perceptions of mathematics. Through biographies, historical figures come to life as a result of the many different anecdotes that help readers paint a picture of individuals' lives that go beyond math.

For example, Paul Erdos couldn't butter his own bread or do his own laundry, yet he was obsessed with math. He also wasn't an introverted or shy mathematician working on formulas all by himself. Instead, Erdos liked working with other mathematicians, actually depending on them, and traveling around the world while relying on the hospitality of fellow mathematicians.

Another recent example can be found in Robbins's *Margaret and the Moon: How Margaret Hamilton Saved the First Lunar Landing* (2017). This book highlights the deep curiosity of Margaret Hamilton, who eventually wrote computer programs that helped NASA land two men on the moon. Hamilton was a curious child, always asking questions and gazing at the night sky, perhaps wondering about the mysteries of space and fascinated by mathematics. Because many youngsters may share her same curiosity, they might feel a personal connection to Hamilton and eventually launch their own dreams.

Math biographies could be read aloud to students or used in literature circles for students to discuss and digest. They also provide possibilities for a reader's theater activity in which students choose one or two pivotal moments in the mathematician's life to dramatize. Alternatively, students might research a mathematician through print and online resources and spend the day dressing, speaking, and acting like him or her. Students might even enjoy convening their own mathematics conference in which attendees debate the importance of a math concept such as prime numbers, circumference, or even pi. Table 8.3 shows a list of quality biographies that could be used in classrooms and their mathematical truths.

In literature circles students could read and prepare ahead of time for their small-group discussion. The nonfiction discussion sheet adapted from Daniels (2002) would be a great tool to get students discussing math literature, specifically biographies (see table 8.4).

When a group of preservice teachers discussed *Lines, Bars and Circles: How William Playfair Invented Graph*s (Becker, 2017) in a math methods class, they first read the book on their own and used the nonfiction discussion sheet to take notes. Then they gathered together to discuss the picture book in a small group. Students were encouraged to begin the discussion with their thoughts and feelings, then use the nonfiction discussion sheet to share their connections, questions, and passages. The goal of the literature discussion was to help everyone make sense of the text, build comprehension, and have fun.

This picture book biography about William Playfair notes that he was a dreamer and joker who looked at the world differently from most scientists or mathematicians. This humorous introduction to the man who believed

Table 8.3. Math Biographies

Title and Author	Mathematical Truths
Ada's Ideas: The Story of Ada Lovelace, the World's First Computer Programmer (Robinson, 2016)	Computer programming
The Boy Who Loved Math: The Impossible Life of Paul Erdos (Heiligman, 2013)	Prime numbers
Lines, Bars and Circles: How William Playfair Invented Graphs (Becker, 2017)	Graphs
Margaret and the Moon: How Margaret Hamilton Saved the First Lunar Landing (Robbins, 2017)	Computer programming
Ticktock: Banneker's Clock (Keller, 2016)	Measurement and time
What's Your Angle, Pythagoras? A Math Adventure (Ellis, 2004)	Geometry, right triangle, Pythagorean theorem
The Librarian Who Measured the Earth (Lasky, 1994)	Measurement
Mathematicians Are People, Too: Stories from the Lives of Great Mathematicians Volume 1 (Reimer & Reimer, 1990)	Thales, Pythagoras, Hypatia, Galileo, Pascal, and others
Pythagoras and the Ratios: A Math Adventure (Ellis, 2010)	Ratios
Blockhead: The Life of Fibonacci (D'Agnese, 2011)	Numbers, patterns, Fibonacci sequence

Table 8.4.   Nonfiction Discussion Sheet Adapted from Daniels (2002)

Your Name:
Book Title:

Connections: What personal math connections did you make with the text? Did it remind you of past mathematical experiences, people, or events in your life?
-
-

Discussion Questions: Jot down two questions. These could be questions that came to your mind while reading, questions you'd like to ask the author, or questions you'd like to investigate or even questions about how to use the book. They could be questions that are directly linked to a mathematical truth of interest in the book or questions that challenge how such truths are represented in the text.
-
-

Passage: What passage about a math concept or mathematical truths jumped out at you as you read the book? These passages may be important, puzzling, beautiful, strange, well written, or controversial. Compare the explanation of a mathematical concept in this passage with an explanation of a similar concept from another source.
-

Application: How could a classroom teacher use this book to teach math? What critical approaches might the classroom teacher adopt in teaching math with this book?
-

Be ready to share all of this information with your literature circle.

numbers and formulas should be presented visually describes how he subsequently created the first line and bar graphs. Even King Louis XVI liked Will's graphs. Yet the scientists during the time period thought Will's pie charts were a distraction and frivolous. It took over one hundred years for graphs and pie charts to catch on. The back matter includes more information about William Playfair with some of his 1786 graphs.

Some of the connections these preservice teachers noted about William Playfair's biography included some surface responses such as "I have an annoying sister and brothers," but others went deeper and saw the impact of a mentor. One student remarked, "I had a great teacher just like Will, who opened my eyes as a student." Many questions arose in their conversation, such as "What is the benefit of portraying Will with constant struggle?" "I wonder if most people desire 'fame, riches, and glory' just like the main character?" and "Why would Will start a business that didn't make him happy?"

The college students discussed how they could use this biography in their future classrooms to introduce graphs. They noted that having students create graphs different from the book for modern twenty-first century inventions would be interesting, "Using a growth mind-set [where effort and time challenges children to learn], kids could redo the graphs in different ways," one said. Plus, all of the students discussed how sharing more historical context on this time period would be fascinating for students. As one asserted, "Tying in a history lesson with this picture book would be fun."

Another small group of preservice teachers discussed *The Boy Who Loved Math: The Impossible Life of Paul Erdos* (Heiligman, 2013). These students asked many questions, such as "What are all of the numbers running across the pages?" "What is the significance of the number one?" and "I wonder why he didn't want to be independent from math?" The students were puzzled by Paul's inability or disinterest in taking care of himself, asking, "Why did his mother keep doing everything for him?" They also asked, "Did his mother probe or encourage higher-order thinking with regard to math since he didn't attend school?"

They moved on to discussing how this picture book biography could be used to complement math instruction. In conclusion, one student emphasized, "A teacher could use this book to discuss history, culture, independence, sharing ideas, working together, and of course prime numbers."

CLASSROOM VIGNETTE

Janet Emmet is a first grade teacher at Saint Joseph's School in Vancouver, Washington. She uses literature and math together because she is convinced that when young children are introduced to topics through stories, they become more engaged and excited about learning. Emmet enjoys connecting literature to as many content areas as possible because students eagerly listen to stories, and she believes it makes learning more relevant to them. She agrees with Raymond (1995), who contends that making connections between mathematics and literature both motivates children to learn mathematics and illustrates the notion that mathematics does not have to be learned "in isolation" from other subject areas.

In addition, Emmet concurs with Whitin (1992) that the teaching and learning of mathematics in today's schools changes dramatically if we view mathematics as a tool for telling stories. Learners see mathematics as a consequence of social interaction; they recognize it as a tool for telling and remembering, not reciting and memorizing.

In Emmet's experience, teaching young children the concepts of place value and regrouping can be difficult. Students must develop a deep understanding of place value concepts in preparation for understanding addition and subtraction beyond basic facts. They must recognize that the digit in the

Box 8.2.

Lesson Plan Using a Children's Book During Math Instruction

Content: The focus for this lesson is on reviewing the concept of considering ten ones as a group or unit called a ten.

Introduction: We will use base ten blocks, specifically rods and units, to review the idea that ten units is equal to one rod. To do this, we will line up the ten units alongside the rod. We will discuss how they are connected.

Main Lesson: We will read and discuss *Ten Apples Up on Top!* (Seuss, 1961). On chart paper, I will have drawings of the characters in the story. As I read aloud the story, I will add the apples to the tops of the characters on the chart paper. At the end of the story, students will be able to recognize that each character has ten apples on his head. They will be able to quickly identify the set of ten apples as one ten. We will then count by tens to determine the total number of apples on the last page of the story.

Follow-Up: Each student will be given one number cube, a stack of apple cutouts, and a large sheet of construction paper. They will roll the die and create sets of ten apples equal to the number rolled on a piece of construction paper. As a class, we will hang up all of the apple stacks and count the total number of apples by tens.

tens place represents groups of tens and the digit in the ones place represents that many ones.

By using picture books and connecting them to symbolic notation, students are able to develop conceptual understanding. Box 8.2 explains one lesson Janet has taught that connects fictional children's literature to mathematics. Teachers could easily replace this text with a nonfiction text.

CONCLUSION

Math is relevant to our students' lives outside of our classrooms. Math and mathematical truths are everywhere, if students only take the time to notice them, and children's literature can complement math instruction and make traditional math class more interesting and relatable to students. Literature may "break down the walls" that children put up about math. Since children and adolescents learn in many different ways, relating literature to math may positively impact math instruction.

Reading aloud or book-talking briefly about a math book are great ways to introduce math concepts. Even having students keep a math journal or vocabulary log in which they record new mathematical terms or concepts they encounter over a period of time as they read, write, and explore the world around them can help them see the relevance of math and begin to understand those mathematical truths.

Lastly, through nonfiction math literature students become more engaged in mathematical concepts. Children's literature is inviting and interesting to young readers because the titles are about experiences to which children can relate. Teachers need to choose quality books that will help students make connections to their own lives, gain mathematical concepts, and make meaning. Through stories, whether fictional or factual, all children can learn. Through well-written math books young readers can discover that mathematics can be an important part of literacy.

REFERENCES

Austin, P. (1998). Math books as literature: Which ones measure up? *New Advocate*, 11(2), 119–133.

Burns, M. (2010). As easy as pi: Picture books are perfect for teaching math. *School Library Journal*, 38–41.

Columba, L., Kim, C. Y., & Moe, A. J. (2005). *The power of picture books in teaching math and science: Grades Pre-K-8*. Scottsdale, AZ: Holcomb Hathaway.

Griffiths, R., & Clyne, M. (1988). *Books you can count on linking mathematics and literature*. Portsmouth, NH: Heinemann.

Daniels, H. (2002). Expository text in literature circles. *Voices from the Middle*, 9(4), 7–14.

Lake, J. (2009). *Math memories you can count on: A literature-based approach to teaching mathematics in the primary grades*. Portland, ME: Stenhouse.

Layne, S. (2009). *Igniting a passion for reading: Successful strategies for building lifelong readers*. Portland, ME: Stenhouse.

McDuffie, A. R., & Young, T. A. (2003). Promoting mathematical discourse through children's literature. *Teaching Children Mathematics*, 9(7), 385–389.

McDuffie, A. R., Young, T. A., & Ward, B. A. (in press). Selecting books to deepen children's understanding of math. In E. E. Monroe & T.A. Young (Eds.), *Deepening students' mathematical understanding with literature*. Reston, VA: National Council of Teachers of Mathematics.

Miller, D. (2009). *The book whisperer: Awakening the inner reader in every child*. San Francisco, CA: Jossey-Bass.

Raymond, A. M. (1995). Engaging young children in mathematical problem solving: providing a context with children's literature. *Contemporary Education, 66*(3), 172–173.

Temple, C .A., Martinez, M., & Yokota, J. (2014). *Children's books in children's hands: A brief introduction to their literature* (5th ed.). New York, NY: Pearson.

Tunnell, M. O., Jacobs, J. S., Young, T. A., & Bryan, G. (2015). *Children's literature, briefly* (6th ed.). New York, NY: Pearson.

Whitin, D. J. (1992). Explore mathematics through children's literature. *School Library Journal*, 24–28.

CHILDREN'S BOOKS CITED

Adler, D. A. (2017). *Let's estimate: A book about estimating and rounding numbers.* Illustrated by E. Miller. New York, NY: Holiday House.

Adler, D. A. (2016). *Place value.* Illustrated by E. Miller. New York, NY: Holiday House.

Becker, H. (2017). *Lines, bars and circles: How William Playfair invented graphs.* Illustrated by M. E. Tremblay. Toronto, ON: Kids Can Press.

Heiligman, D. (2013). *The boy who loved math: The improbable life of Paul Erdos.* Illustrated by L. Pham. New York, NY: Roaring Brook Press.

Nagda, A. W., & Bickel, C. (2000). *Tiger math: Learning to graph from a baby tiger.* New York, NY: Macmillan.

Robbins, D. (2017). *Margaret and the moon: How Margaret Hamilton saved the first lunar landing.* Illustrated by L. Knisley. New York, NY: Knopf Books for Young Readers.

Seuss, G. (1961). *Ten apples up on top!* Illustrated by R. McKie. New York, NY: Random House.

Chapter Nine

Some Nonfiction Resources for Engaging in Critical Conversations

Chris Landauer, Cheryl Logan,
and René Rodríguez-Astacio

WHY CRITICAL CONVERSATIONS ABOUT NONFICTION?

When choosing nonfiction texts, it has always been essential to identify reliable sources of information. That point has been further illuminated in the current political climate where there have been many unsubstantiated claims made that seem aimed to distract and obscure truth by creating a moving target of information. In an effort to seek credible information, people are often confronted by a lot of misinformation.

This is complicated by the fact that there are a multitude of websites, no matter how unreliable, that provide content that exploits people's confirmation bias. Teachers, then, play a significant role in ensuring that students develop strong information literacy skills and in guiding them toward authentic sources of nonfiction literature.

What follows next is a series of nonfiction resources compiled to guide educators navigating the overabundance of content that can be found on the Internet and elsewhere, some of which contains information that not only is unreliable, but also erodes efforts to seek truth. It should be noted that it is important to not only have access to reliable information, but more fundamentally, it is imperative that students are guided to construct their own knowledge and given opportunities to think critically so they can learn how to identify information that is inaccurate or incomplete.

Still, by writing this chapter, it is the hope that this collection of resources can be a helpful tool in educators' classrooms as they attempt to engage students in critical conversations about historical and current events in the world.

WHAT IS CRITICAL LITERACY AND WHY
IS IT IMPORTANT WHEN READING NONFICTION?

Critical literacy means actively and reflectively reading. Critical literacy invites questioning and capitalizes on human beings' natural curiosity. Rather than stifling that human impulse to know more, teachers embracing critical literacy encourage their students to challenge the information shared in their classrooms.

Deeper questioning of a nonfiction text reveals a more fully formed picture of what is being conveyed. Critical literacy often involves challenging the status quo and demands thinking about how power dynamics influence the ideas within a text. In doing so, critical literacy helps students learn how to work against injustice by not allowing problematic ideas to go unchallenged.

It is important for students to approach each nonfiction text they encounter with a critical lens, to question the source of the information, to think about the time and context in which the information was written, and to look for unspoken ideas or implicit biases that may be embedded within the text. When a student is provided an informational text, without critical literacy they may just take the words at face value.

By thinking about the lens from which a nonfiction text was written and by knowing it is okay and even expected that they ask questions, students will develop the instinct to actively engage with material, reflect on ideas they encounter, and then, if necessary, challenge what they are reading rather than inattentively accepting everything they are told.

In this sense, all nonfiction texts can have some value because students will have the tools to distinguish between factually accurate texts and those that contain misinformation. Nevertheless, the resources listed are considered more valuable because they provide information deemed to be reliable, informative, and therefore helpful for teachers in promoting critical conversations in their classrooms.

NONFICTION ONLINE RESOURCES

Zinn Education Project, zinnedproject.org

This free resource was founded by William Holtzman, a former student of historian and social activist Howard Zinn, as a tool for teachers to extend Zinn's work of reexamining how history is taught in schools, recentering how students learn about the past through the lens of those whose stories have been traditionally left out of school textbooks. In doing so, the Zinn Education Project invites students to think more critically and presents learners with a more nuanced and truthful account of the history of the United States than they would otherwise be likely to encounter in their schooling.

The materials provided within this resource highlight how people of color, women, and working people have played a significant part in social movements that have shaped the world. Instead of history being taught as a way of celebrating a select group of "elite" individuals, the Zinn Education Project centers on the way "everyday" people have come together to create change in the world, an approach that invites students to see themselves as having the ability to impact change. Educational materials are free and easy to find through the ability to search by time period, theme, and resource type.

Resources can also be sorted by reading level. Two other organizations, Teaching for Change (teachingforchange.org) and Rethinking Schools (rethinkingschools.org), which each predated the Zinn Education Project, coordinate the Zinn Education Project and are also incredibly valuable resources in and of themselves.

Teaching for Change: Building Social Justice Starting in the Classroom, teachingforchange.org

As mentioned above, Teaching for Change is one of the organizations, along with Rethinking Schools, that manages the Zinn Education Project. In addition to that, though, there are many other resources that can be found within Teaching for Change that are valuable tools for educators. For example, there is an Anti-Bias Education section that offers recommended booklists; an extensive collection of materials from which teachers can draw, in both English and Spanish; as well as materials with which families can engage.

Additionally, the website coordinates various other projects that branch from their site including, to name a couple, a Civil Rights Teaching section, which links to a project they have developed to educate students about civil rights movements, and a Teaching Central America section, which links to another project they created with lesson plans and recommended books to educate students about, among other things, global interconnectedness and how U.S. foreign policy decisions have influenced immigration patterns from Central America to the United States.

Teaching Tolerance: A Project by the Southern Poverty Law Center, tolerance.org

This free resource was founded by the Southern Poverty Law Center to promote equity in schools by providing materials for educators to use in their classrooms. There are many lesson plans that are easy to find through the search function that allows you to sort by grade level, topic, and subject area. There are also webinars, professional development references, and film kits available, as well as a triannual magazine that can be downloaded for free.

National Council of Teachers of English, ncte.org/lessons/nonfiction-texts

The National Council of Teacher of English (NCTE), an organization dedicated to the improvement of teaching and learning English, provides a space with lesson plans and strategies for teachers of K-12 levels interested in teaching content-rich nonfiction and informational texts. It also includes strategy guides on activities such as I-search writing, concept sorts for vocabulary building, how to build connections (text-to-text, text-to-self, and text-to-world), and seed discussions. Lessons and strategies listed in here are also part of NCTE's partnership with ReadWriteThink, an organization focused on providing parents and educators with free high-quality teaching materials.

ReadWriteThink, http://www.readwritethink.org/

This organization offers parents, teachers, and after-school programs free high-quality lessons on reading and language arts instruction. It also offers a wide array of materials such as lesson plans for units and mini-lessons, assessment tools, podcasts, professional journal articles, and book titles. Per the organization's standard, lesson plans available in this website are aligned to the Common Core State Standards and individual state standards. Moreover, this organization works in collaboration with the National Council of Teachers of English and the International Literacy Association.

Reading Rockets, readingrockets.org

This website is a national literacy initiative that offers teachers, parents, librarians, and everyone who works with children who are learning to read become strong readers. Their goal is to spread the word about research in reading instruction through strategies and reading materials that anyone can use and understand. The project includes PBS television programs, classroom strategies, opportunities for professional development, a robust community through social media, and access to services through their own website and ColorinColorado.org.

The website also features a section titled "Children's Books & Authors" that includes author interviews, themed booklists, and a section on nonfiction literature for children. In 2016, Reading Rockets received the David M. Rubenstein Prize from the Library of Congress Literacy Award Program.

Smithsonian Tween Tribune, https://www.tweentribune.com/, and Newsela, https://newsela.com/

These two websites offer articles from major news publications adapted for a variety of reading levels and abilities. They each also provide teachers with tools created for use in specific subject areas. Both websites offer teachers the opportunity to register and assign readings, quizzes, critical thinking questions, and annotations to their students through either a web browser or their mobile application. While Smithsonian Tween Tribune is free to join, Newsela has both a free section and a paid PRO section with some enhancements. These two websites offer content in both English and Spanish.

Nonfiction Booklist: Diverse Nonfiction Literature for Young Readers, nonfictionbooklist.com

This project aims to create a booklist of nonfiction literature for young readers. The nonfiction books listed here focus on stories centered on people of color. As such, the website features a drop-down menu that allows for searches based on ethnicities, age, and subject. This project is led by Dr. Lauren Causey and it is funded by the Carnegie-Whitney Grant from the American Library Association.

NONFICTION PRINT RESOURCES

Dorman, L. R., & Cappelli, R. (2009). *Nonfiction mentor text: Teaching informational writing through children's literature*. Portland, ME: Stenhouse Publishers.

    This practical text provides teachers with detailed lessons plans for teaching K-8 students how to craft effective nonfiction writing. This resource offers a variety of nonfiction children's texts that serve as mentor texts for teachers to utilize in instruction in the writing workshop.

Lehman, B. (2007). Literary learning and the whole curriculum. In *Children's Literature and Learning: Literary Study Across the Curriculum* (pp. 57–68). New York, NY: Teachers College Press.

    This text provides teachers with the theoretical underpinnings on the literary qualities found in informational texts. Further, this text provides instructional methods for literary teaching of children's nonfiction across the curriculum.

Kiefer, B. (2010). Nonfiction books. In *Charlotte Huck's children's literature* (10th ed). (pp. 492–507). Boston, MA: McGraw-Hill Higher Education.

   This chapter provides teachers with an in-depth explanation of the genre of nonfiction including a brief history of the trends in nonfiction books. In addition, Kiefer offers criteria for evaluating books for accuracy and authenticity, content and perspective, style and organization, as well as illustrations and format. Included in this chapter is an exploration of ideas for engaging students in evaluating and critiquing nonfiction texts. Further, an extensive list of nonfiction titles for children, web links for teachers, and related professional readings make this chapter a highly valuable resource for teachers and students working with nonfiction texts.

WHAT AWARDS EXIST THAT CAN
HELP WITH DISCUSSIONS ABOUT NONFICTION?

In the early years of children's and young adult literature, nonfiction was an undervalued genre in the body of literature for young people. In fact, only six nonfiction children's and young adult titles were recognized as worthy of receiving the Newbery Medal between the 1920s and 1980s (*The Story of Mankind* [1921] by Hendrik Willem van Loon; *Invincible Louisa: The Story of the Author of Little Women* [1933] by Cornelia Megs; *Daniel Boone* [1939] by James Daugherty; *Amos Fortune, Free Man* [1950] by Elizabeth Yates; *Carry On, Mr. Bowditch* [1955] by Jean Lee Latham; and *Lincoln: A Photobiography* [1987] by Russell Freedman).

   In an effort to increase the number of nonfiction titles available for young people, the National Council of Teachers of English established the Orbis Pictus Award in 1989 to recognize authors whose work exemplified excellence in writing nonfiction for children. The Association for Library Service to Children later established the Sibert Award in 2001 to honor a distinguished informational book published in the previous year. These and other notable awards help teachers in selecting high-quality texts to engage children in critical thinking and discussion.

NONFICTION-SPECIFIC AWARDS

Orbis Pictus Award, ncte.org/awards/orbispictus

Established by the National Council of Teachers of English in 1989, the Orbis Pictus Award is one of the most prestigious awards that can be given to a nonfiction book. This annual award is given to an author in recognition of excellence in writing of nonfiction literature for children published in the United States.

Robert F. Sibert Award, ala.org/alsc/ awardsgrants/bookmedia/sibertmedal

Established in 2001, in honor of Robert F. Sibert, this award is given by the Association for Library Service to Children (ALSC) to an author and illustrator in recognition of a notable informational text published in English in the United States in the previous year.

Boston Globe-Horn Book Awards, hbook.com/bghb/index.php

Established in 1967, the Boston Globe-Horn Book Awards is one of the most renowned awards in children's and young adult literature. In the spring of each year, books in three categories (Poetry, Picture Book, and Nonfiction) are recognized for their excellence in children's and young adult literature.

Eureka Awards, californiareads.org/display.asp?p=awards_eureka

Established by the California Reading Association, this award recognizes and honors nonfiction books for children.

The Children's Book Guild—Nonfiction Award, childrensbookguild.org/nonfiction-award/criteria

Awarded by the Children's Book Guild of Washington, DC, this award recognizes a living author or author-illustrator whose work has significantly contributed to the quality of nonfiction for children.

YALSA Nonfiction Award, http://www.ala.org/ yalsa/nonfiction-award

Established in 2010, the Young Adult Library Services Association (YALSA) annually recognizes a "best" nonfiction text written for young adults for its excellence in nonfiction.

Outstanding Science Trade Book Award, http://www.nsta.org/publications/ostb/

The Outstanding Science Trade Book Award recognizes outstanding children's science trade books for children in grades K-12. The books are selected by the National Science Teachers Association (NSTA) in cooperation with the Children's Book Council (CBC).

OTHER LITERATURE AWARDS

In addition to the awards that specifically honor nonfiction literature written for young people, teachers may also find notable and excellent nonfiction titles among other children's and young adult literature awards. The following awards provide teachers with lists of high-quality literature that can include nonfiction titles for children and young adults.

Caldecott Medal Award, http://www.ala.org/awardsgrants/randolph-caldecott-medal-1

The Caldecott Medal is awarded annually to an illustrator for eminence in illustrations in an American picture book for children.

Coretta Scott King Award, http://www.ala.org/emiert/cskbookawards

Awarded annually in honor of the life and work of Dr. Martin Luther King Jr., this award is given to an African American author and illustrator whose work makes an outstanding contribution to the African American experience.

Jane Addams Children's Book Award, janeaddamspeace.org/jacba/

Awarded annually to a children's book published in the preceding year for its literary merit and for effectively promoting children's thinking and discussion of equity, peace, dignity, social justice, and global community. The award has been presented annually since 1953 by the Women's International League for Peace and Freedom and the Jane Addams Peace Association.

Pura Belpré Award, http://www.ala.org/alsc/awardsgrants/bookmedia/belpremedal

Established in 1996, this award was named after the first Latina librarian in the New York Public Library and is given annually to a Latino/Latina author and illustrator whose work excellently portrays the Latino culture and experience.

American Indian Youth Services Literature Award, ailanet.org/activities/american-indian-youth-literature-award/

Established in 2006, this award is given every two years to a Native American author and illustrator whose work authentically represents the Native American experience and culture, historically and present day.

Asian Pacific American Awards for Literature, http://www. apalaweb.org/awards/literature-awards/

This award is given to Asian/Pacific American authors and illustrators for excellence in literary and artistic merit and for excellence in portraying the Asian/Pacific American culture and experience.

The Schneider Family Book Award, ala.org/awardsgrants/ schneider-family-book-award

Established in 2003, the Schneider Family Book Award annually recognizes books that authentically represent characters' experiences with disabilities. This award recognizes books on three levels: Teen Book, Middle School Book, and Children's Book.

Mildred Batchelder Award, ala.org/alsc/awardsgrants/bookmedia/ batchelderaward

Sponsored by the Association for Library Service to Children, this award is given to an American publisher for outstanding books originally published in a foreign language and later translated in English and published in the United States.

Odyssey Award, ala.org/ALSC/ awardsgrants/bookmedia/odysseyaward

Awarded by the Association for Library Service to Children, this award recognizes a producer for the best audiobook produced for children and/or young adults in any genre.

CONCLUSION

This chapter is intended to serve as a useful catalog in the toolkit of educators that are looking to create a critically engaged classroom environment.

This list of resources is by no means comprehensive, but it can play a role in directing educators toward resources that will stimulate critical conversations in classrooms and schools across the country. Students and teachers do not learn or teach in a bubble. Schools exist within communities.

What happens outside of the school impacts what happens in school, and vice versa. Schools must play a role in ensuring that students are critically engaged with what is happening in their communities and in the world. Nonfiction literature provides an excellent avenue to foster this engagement. As teachers are able to effectively utilize nonfiction resources and embrace critical literacy in their classrooms, they will help prepare students to be engaged citizens who know how to identify and challenge injustice and oppression in the world.

About the Editors

Vivian Yenika-Agbaw is professor of children's literature in the Department of Curriculum and Instruction at the Pennsylvania State University, University Park, where she teaches undergraduate and graduate courses in children's/adolescent literature. She has published numerous articles and authored/coedited several books including *Adolescents Rewrite Their Worlds: Using Literature to Illustrate Writing Forms* (Rowman & Littlefield, 2015); *African Youth in Contemporary Literature and Popular Culture: Identity Quest* (2014); and *Fairy Tales with a Black Consciousness: Essays on Adaptations of Familiar Stories* (2013). She has taught children's literature in the Departments of Curriculum and Instruction and English at state universities in Pennsylvania (Clarion and Bloomsburg) and has taught high school English abroad and in the United States. Yenika-Agbaw has served on several editorial boards and reviewed manuscripts for *Children's Literature in Education*, *Children's Literature*, and *Journal of Children's Literature*. She is currently serving on the International Research Society for Children's Literature Board (2017–2019).

Laura Anne Hudock is a PhD candidate in curriculum and instruction at the Pennsylvania State University, where she instructs preservice teachers in children's literature, reading, and language arts courses. She also teaches in Penn State's World Campus program on the art of picture books and fantasy children's literature. Hudock has presented papers at national and international conferences on picture books and reader responses to them. In 2016, she co-authored a chapter with Dr. Dan Hade, "Redefining the Early Reader in an Era of Multiliteracies: Visual Language of Mo Willems' Elephant and Piggie Series," in *The Early Reader in Children's Literature and Culture: Theorizing Books for Beginning Readers*, edited by Miskec and Wannamaker. Previously,

Hudock taught first grade for a decade in Virginia at a Title I elementary school and in Florida.

Ruth McKoy Lowery is professor of literacy and associate chair of the Department of Teaching and Learning at the Ohio State University. She teaches courses on children's literature and literacy education. Her current research focuses on children's literature—particularly immigrant and multicultural literature, the adaptation of immigrant and at-risk students in schools, and preparing teachers to teach a diverse student population. Lowery is an active member of the National Council of Teachers of English (NCTE), the International Literacy Association (ILA), and the United States Board on Books for Young People (USBBY).

About the Contributors

Shanetia P. Clark, PhD, is an associate professor of literacy in the Department of Teacher Education at Salisbury University (Maryland). She holds a bachelor's degree in English and a master's in teaching degree from the University of Virginia. She attended graduate school at the Pennsylvania State University, where she earned a PhD in curriculum and instruction, with an emphasis in language and literacy education. Her interests include young adult and children's literature, the exploration of aesthetic experiences within reading and writing classrooms, and writing pedagogy. She has published peer-reviewed articles and book chapters within these professional interests. She has published in journals such as the *Journal of Language and Literacy*, *International Journal of Learning*, the *ALAN Review*, and the *SIGNAL Journal*. She teaches courses in children's literature, creative arts in literacy, and language arts methods. In addition, Clark supervises interns in local schools.

Deanna Day teaches undergraduate and graduate literacy and technology courses for Washington State University. She has served on the Notable Children's Books in the Language Arts award and the Notable Books for Global Society committees. She also reviews children's literature for *The Dragon Lode*.

Vincent Genareo is an assistant professor of educational psychology at Salisbury University in Salisbury, Maryland. He received his PhD in teaching and learning from the University of North Dakota. His background is as a classroom teacher and, later, in educational assessment and evaluation. Genareo prepares future and current teachers in assessment methods and pedagogical design. His research interests include K-12 STEM pedagogy and assessment, curriculum-based measurement in mathematics, and the influence of university partnership programs on K-12 students' STEM interests.

Xenia Hadjioannou is associate professor of language and literacy education at the Harrisburg campus of Penn State University. A former elementary teacher, Hadjioannou holds a bachelor's degree in the sciences of education from the University of Cyprus, a master of education from the University of Florida, and a PhD in instruction and curriculum also from the University of Florida.

In her teaching, Hadjioannou works with pre- and in-service teachers in various courses on language and literacy methodology. Her research focuses on the study of classroom discourse that supports student thinking and learning; the analysis of exemplary practices in the language arts classroom; and the preparation of teachers to effectively work with diverse students, including emergent bilinguals. Hadjioannou's work has appeared in various journals such as the *American Educational Research Journal*, the *Early Education and Development Journal*, *The Dragon Lode*, and the *International Journal of Multicultural Education*.

Chris Landauer is a PhD candidate at the Ohio State University, focusing on multicultural and equity studies in education, as well as social studies and global education. Landauer also works as a graduate teaching associate. His current research looks at how preservice teachers are thinking about issues related to social justice and the role that social justice will play in their future classrooms. Prior to his current role at Ohio State, Landauer spent ten years as a high school teacher.

Cheryl Logan is an instructor and second-year doctoral student in literature for children and young adults in the Department of Teaching and Learning at the Ohio State University. Logan's research interests include representations of African American boys and African American boyhood in children's literature. Logan has eighteen years of teaching experience in language arts and youth literature. Currently, she teaches courses in literature for adolescents, children's literature, and multicultural education to preservice educators.

L. J. Phillips is an English and drama teacher at an all-girls school just outside Toronto, Canada. She spends her days surrounded by teenage girls who provide excellent material for her creative writing and inspire new innovations in the classroom. When she's not marking or directing various dramatic productions, Phillips enjoys nothing more than reading and writing about books on mychildhoodbookshelf.com, and in the summer, she travels to exotic locations ticking one item off her bucket list each year. Phillips recently completed her master of education focusing on children's literature at Penn State and is currently planning to further her studies in this area.

Elizabeth Raff is an innovative, passionate, and enthusiastic educator who sparks excitement and creativity in her classroom. A sixth grade teacher from Pennsylvania, Raff propels students to be lifelong learners by using unique classroom engagement strategies. She creates a model classroom with high expectations and a student-driven culture where students are encouraged to ask tough questions and think outside of the box.

When she is not in the classroom, Raff, an inspiring educator, develops comprehensive curriculum, leads energizing professional development workshops, and supports preservice teachers. Raff's classroom techniques are being utilized around the world and most recently gained the attention of Pennsylvania's secretary of education, Pedro Rivera. She received her master of education in curriculum and instruction from Penn State University and continues to pursue research and writing opportunities.

René M. Rodríguez-Astacio is a PhD candidate from the Pennsylvania State University. His area of emphasis is in English language arts and children's literature, and his research interests fall within the area of multicultural children's and young adult's literature. He also advocates toward LGBTIQ+ and multicultural representation within the field of children's literature. Rodríguez-Astacio has published book reviews about music-themed picture books in the spring 2017 issue of *The Dragon Lode*, as well as collaborative poetry, "The Disenfranchised Learner," in the *Journal of Language and Literacy Education*. In addition, he has presented his research in multicultural literature at conferences such as the 2016 NCTE Annual Convention and the 2017 Children's Literature Association Conference.

Nancy Rankie Shelton, professor, literacy education, conducts research in urban elementary school settings focusing on the ways in which schools prepare literate, participatory citizens for the twenty-first century. She has created and sustained long-term partnerships with schools in Baltimore City, where she works with faculty and students to provide enriching, literate classroom environments and school-based professional development.

She is an active member of the National Council of Teachers of English (NCTE) and the Center for Expansion of Language and Thinking (CELT).

Her two most current publications are *5-13: A Memoir of Love, Loss and Survival* (2016), which shares the experience of her husband's diagnosis with stage IV cancer and his death (http://www.5-13amemoir.com), and *Literacy Policies and Practices in Conflict: Reclaiming Classrooms in Networked Times* (2015) which examines the tensions between federal policy and effective classroom practices and how those tensions impact the learning experiences of students.

Melissa Stewart is the award-winning author of more than 180 nonfiction books for children, including *Can an Aardvark Bark?*, illustrated by Caldecott honoree Steve Jenkins; *No Monkeys, No Chocolate*, illustrated by Nicole Wong; and *Feathers: Not Just for Flying*, illustrated by Sarah S. Brannen. She is the coauthor, with Nancy Chesley, of *Perfect Pairs: Using Fiction and Nonfiction Picture Books to Teach Life Science, K-2*, and *Perfect Pairs: Using Fiction and Nonfiction Picture Books to Teach Life Science, Grades 3-5* and has written articles about teaching nonfiction reading and writing for *AASL Knowledge Quest, Book Links, Reading Today, School Library Connection, Science, Science Books & Films*, and the Two Writing Teachers and Nerdy Book Club blogs. Stewart's highly regarded website features a rich array of educational resources for teaching nonfiction reading and writing: www.melissa-stewart.com.

An avid reader, **Barbara A. Ward** is an associate clinical professor of literacy and children's literature at Washington State University in Pullman, where she coordinates the elementary education program. She spent twenty-five years teaching in the public schools of New Orleans, Louisiana.

For over ten years, **Marnie Woodley** has been teaching a range of science and social science courses in the middle and high school classrooms. She spends her days working with diverse groups of students who challenge her to continually innovate and differentiate her teaching methods. Recently she has expanded her teaching role to include professional development opportunities for her colleagues, presenting seminars and workshops regarding the use of effective teaching and learning strategies in the classroom. Woodley lives just outside Toronto, Canada, with her husband and very busy twin girls who continually remind her of the value of asking "why?"

Terrell A. Young is professor of children's literature at the David O. McKay School of Education at Brigham Young University in Provo, Utah. Young is a coauthor or coeditor of numerous books on children's literature, including *Deepening Students' Mathematical Understanding with Children's Litera-*

ture (in press), *Children's Literature, Briefly* (2016), *Integrating Children's Literature through the Common Core State Standards* (2015), and *Independent Reading: Creating Lifelong Readers* (2015). He previously taught in public elementary schools in Utah and Wyoming and private elementary schools in Venezuela. Young has served as president of the ILA Children's Literature and Reading Special Interest Group and the NCTE Children's Literature Assembly. He is currently the president-elect of the United States Board on Books for Young People. Young has enjoyed serving on numerous award committees, and was recently elected to serve on the 2019 Newbery Award Selection Committee.

www.ingramcontent.com/pod-product-compliance
Lightning Source LLC
Chambersburg PA
CBHW070911030726
47504CB00005B/1557